From Many Books: a Lifetime of Recipes

Lorraine McFadden

Library and Archives Canada Cataloguing in Publication

McFadden, Lorraine

From Many Books: A Lifetime of Recipes

ISBN: 978-1-9991876-0-6

Published by Lorraine McFadden

Cover design and layout by Daria Lacy

Cover photo by Emre Can

Edited by Sarina Cornthwaite

Acknowledgements

for Bill

With many thanks to the Test Kitchen Committee:

Wendy Davis

Connie Marshall

Carol-Anne Noble

Liz Palwick-Goebel

Judith Warren

Despite editing and testing, it's cooking and things can go awry.
Any errors in the recipes are mine alone.

Foreword

When I was ten years old, my mother was laid up in hospital with an injury. During her recovery, I started cooking for my father and brother. There was no one else available to teach me how to make dinners, and so I became a self-taught cook, by necessity. I think there was one cookbook in the kitchen, an old Purity Flour cookbook given to my mother when she married. There was also a collection of spice bottles of the same vintage. We lived in a small village in Quebec, with one supermarket and no other source of groceries. I was on my own. I loved it.

I have cooked a lot of dishes and tried many recipes since I was 10 years old. I have recipes copied out in both a little girl's hand and a young woman's script, later printed with a busy professional woman's photocopier and printer. Friends have gifted me with their best recipes. I grew up in Ontario and Quebec, have lived abroad, and travelled around some. I have bought a lot of cookbooks, borrowed some from libraries, and yearned for the volumes in my mother in law's massive collection.

This is my distilled experience. As these recipes cover a lifetime, they reflect the learning curve of a novice cook (Never Fail Pastry), and changing preferences in this generation for less sugar (Peach Pie), less processed food (make your own bread) and more vegetables.

I hope you find many dishes here you enjoy making and eating.

By the way, you'll see a few branded products in the recipes. I only put them in when there is no generic equivalent, and it is the product I use when I make the recipe. No one has asked me to do this, and I do not get paid a product placement fee. It's on the house.

Lorraine McFadden
June 2019
London Ontario

Common Abbreviations

tsp	= teaspoon
tbsp	= tablespoon
oz	= ounce
ml	= millilitre
li	= litre (1000 ml)
F	= Fahrenheit
C	= Celsius

Volume Measurement Conversions

liquids by volume:

3 teaspoons	= 1 tablespoon	= 1/2 fluid ounce
2 tablespoons	= 1/8 cup	= 1 fluid ounce
4 tablespoons	= 1/4 cup	= 2 fluid ounces
8 tablespoons	= 1/2 cup	= 4 fluid ounces
1 cup	= 1/2 pint	= 8 fluid ounces
1 pint	= 2 cups	= 16 fluid ounces
4 cups	= 1 quart	= 32 fluid ounces
4 quarts	= 1 gallon	= 128 fluid ounces

Imperial to metric volumes:

1 teaspoon	= 5 ml
1 tablespoon	= 15 ml
1 fluid ounce	= 30 ml
1/5 cup	= 50 ml
1 cup	= 240 ml
2 cups (1 pint)	= 470 ml
4 cups (1 quart)	= 950 ml
4 quarts (1 gallon)	= 3.8 li
1 ounce	= 28 grams
3.5 ounces	= 100 grams

1 pound	= 454 grams
35 ounces	= 1 kilogram (1000 grams)
2.205 pounds	= 1 kilogram (1000 grams)

Oven Temperature Conversions

275 F	= 140 C	gas mark 1
300 F	= 150 C	gas mark 2
325 F	= 165 C	gas mark 3
350 F	= 180 C	gas mark 4
375 F	= 190 C	gas mark 5
400 F	= 200 C	gas mark 6
425 F	= 220 C	gas mark 7
450 F	= 230 C	gas mark 9
475 F	= 240 C	gas mark 10

Imperial to metric weight conversions

1 ounce	= 28 g
4 ounces (1/4 pound)	= 113 g
1/3 pound	= 150 g
8 ounces (1/2 pound)	= 230 g
2/3 pound	= 300 g
12 ounces (3/4 pound)	= 340 g
1 pound (16 ounces)	= 450 g
2 pounds	= 900 g

Approximate Conversion Flour Volume to Weight

(recipes in this book only use all purpose flour, but flour weight can vary)

1 cup all purpose flour   = 120 grams   = 4 1/4 ounces

Chapter 1

Appetizers

My favourite way to entertain is a table or kitchen island laid out with appetizers and finger foods, so that I can stop when the dishes and drinks are prepared and enjoy the guests. Many of these recipes can be made ahead and cooked or set out in the last hour before serving.

Smoked Salmon Rolls

When I bring these to a family function, my sister in law smiles happily, and lingers next to them at the buffet table. Make these ahead of time, then wrap well without slicing and store in the refrigerator. When you are ready to serve, unwrap and slice diagonally and lay them out in a spoke pattern on a serving plate.

1 package of 10 large plain or whole wheat tortillas

2 8 ounce packages cream cheese, softened to room temperature

500 gm thinly sliced smoked salmon

1/2 cup capers, drained

1 small red onion, finely chopped

Take a wrap and spread a thin layer of cream cheese almost to the edge. Place strips of smoked salmon to cover. Sprinkle capers and red onion on top, roll and wrap tightly. At this point, you can refrigerate them until ready to serve. Slice the rolls on a diagonal, for pieces about 3 inches long. Trim off edges that have no filling. Lay out decoratively on a plate.

Pop's Potted Cheese

Early on in our relationship I discovered Bill loves very old, crumbly, cheddar cheese, so I started looking for ways to use it in the kitchen. I found this easy-to-make recipe in Cathy Prange and Joan Pauli's *Nifty Nibbles* (1983). I made it by hand before I had a food processor, but a processor would work well. You can make it ahead and store in the refrigerator. Let it come up to room temperature before serving, as that improves the cheddar flavour.

1 lb old cheddar cheese, grated

1/4 cup minced green onion tops

1 tbsp Dijon mustard

1 ounce cognac, brandy or dry sherry

2 tbsp butter, softened

Combine cheese and onion tops. Gradually blend in mustard, cognac and butter. Stir until smooth. Add more butter until it is easy to spread. Pack into small containers and wrap with plastic wrap. It can be stored in the refrigerator, but allow to come to room temperature to serve.

Brandied Chicken Liver Pate

I like to put out richer, high protein finger foods at parties to balance out the drinks. This is from Carol Ferguson's *The Canadian Living Cookbook*. It is a good make-ahead appetizer, and benefits from a little time to mellow out the flavours. This recipe makes about 2 cups (500 ml).

1 lb chicken livers

2 tbsp butter

2 cloves garlic, minced

1 small onion, chopped

1/4 cup brandy

1/2 tsp salt

pinch (1/8 tsp) each of pepper, cloves and allspice

1/2 cup chicken stock

1/2 cup butter, softened

Cut livers in half. Melt 2 tbsp butter in a skillet. Cook livers just until no pink colour remains in their centres. Add garlic and onion; stir and cook lightly. Stir in the brandy, salt, pepper, cloves and allspice. In a food processor or blender, combine chicken liver mixture, stock and softened butter. Blend until very smooth. Check seasonings, and adjust if necessary. Pour into a small crock or bowl. Cover tightly and refrigerate for several hours, until it is a spreadable consistency.

Spiced Nuts

Last year, we held a Christmas open house. Some friends are vegetarian, while others are vegan, and I wanted to be sure there would be a lot of choices for them. I added a small scoop to the serving bowl and a pile of paper cups or tart liners, so that people could serve themselves a portion and carry it around. This recipe is also from Carol Ferguson's *The Canadian Living Cookbook.*

Preheat oven to 350F.

Mix together in a large bowl:

4 cups nuts	1 tbsp Dijon mustard
1 tbsp olive oil	

Mix together in a separate bowl:

2 tbsp brown sugar	1 tsp salt
1 tbsp dry mustard	1/2 tsp chili powder
1 1/2 tsp ground coriander	1/4 tsp pepper

Mix contents of both bowls together. Bake on parchment paper for 15 – 17 minutes. Stir once. Don't let it go beyond 17 minutes; it will burn by 20 minutes.

Boursin Mushrooms on Puff Pastry

I found this on the Boursin website. It is one of the very few products I'll specify by name, but there is no adequate substitute. This is an impressive appetizer. It is not a make ahead dish; puff pastry deflates over time and is less tasty when cool. Put it in the oven just ahead of when you want to serve it. It is absolutely worth it.

1/2 package frozen puff pastry, thawed

1 pint white mushrooms

1 tbsp oil

salt and pepper to taste

1 package of garlic herb Boursin cheese

1/2 tsp each dried rosemary & thyme

Preheat oven to 400F. Slice mushrooms and sauté with a sprinkle of salt, pepper and thyme. Cook until mushrooms are browned. When they release a small amount of liquid, sprinkle in the rosemary and thyme. Cook a few minutes longer, then remove from heat. Roll out the pastry into a rectangle about 8" x 20". Spread mushrooms over the pastry, leaving a one and a half inch edge. Crumble Boursin over the top of the mushrooms. Bake for 15 – 20 minutes until pastry is puffed and golden. Serve warm in slices or wedges.

Pigs in Blankets

The combination of mustard, garlic sausages and puff pastry is magic. Like the Boursin mushrooms, these should be put in the oven just before serving. However, all the prep work can be done days ahead, as the sausage rolls go in the freezer and cook straight from frozen. I have adapted the recipe slightly from the Martha Stewart website.

1 package of frozen puff pastry from a good European style deli

Honey Dijon mustard

18 cooked sausages: I recommend garlic Polish sausages

1 large egg, beaten

coarse salt

Roll out puff pastry and cut in 4 or 5 inch squares, depending on the length of the sausage. Brush bottom edge, about 2 inches deep, of each square with mustard. Place 1 sausage on bottom edge of pastry on top of the mustard. Roll up and press pastry together tightly to seal. Brush top with egg and then sprinkle with salt. Continue until all the puff pastry has been used. You can make these ahead of time and freeze the wrapped sausages at this point.

To cook, place frozen sausages on parchment paper lined baking sheets. Preheat oven to 400F. Bake until puffed and golden brown, about 25 minutes. Serve warm with extra mustard.

Chapter 2

Soup

It was years before I learned to make good soup. Good soup requires a good stock and my early efforts with bouillon cubes were disappointing. I find making stock from scratch time consuming, and the results were sometimes bland, so I now rely on stock base in jars. There are only a few recipes in this section, but that is progress.

Vegetable Soup

This soup happened in the middle of winter, when the bell pepper was showing its first wrinkles and it was time to use up the tomatoes. I like soups with a little more body in colder months, and the last chunk of Boursin was the answer.

2 tbsp extra virgin olive oil

1 green pepper

3 stalks celery

1 onion

6 medium ripe tomatoes

2 cups chicken stock (I like the Better Than Bouillon brand, but make the stock a little richer by adding more stock paste)

1/4 of 150 gm package garlic herb Boursin cheese

Chop the pepper, celery and onion. sauté in oil in a large stock pot. Quarter, core, de-seed and chop 6 tomatoes. Add chopped fresh tomatoes and chicken stock to the sautéed vegetables. Bring to a gentle boil. As the tomatoes cook, mash them up with a potato masher. Add in the garlic herb Boursin cheese. Stir to melt. Let soup simmer until everything is cooked well. Serve hot.

Cream of Mushroom Soup

One winter weekend, I was shopping at the local farmer's market looking for some mushrooms. It was late in the day and the shopkeeper made me an offer on all their organic mushrooms that I couldn't refuse. It was time to make mushroom soup and invite some friends over. I looked up a recipe from *Mark Bittman's How to Cook Everything*, and adapted it slightly for the ingredients I had on hand. Come dinnertime, there were six of us around the table and hardly a word was spoken. It's very gratifying when people are too busy spooning your meal up to talk.

1 lb fresh mushrooms, cleaned, trimmed and sliced

2 tbsp butter or extra virgin olive oil

salt and freshly ground pepper to taste

2 tbsp minced shallots

1 tsp minced garlic

3 cups mushroom broth (I use Better Than Bouillon mushroom base)

1 cup light cream (5%), half and half (10%) or heavy cream

Place the butter or oil in a large, deep pan and turn the heat on to medium. When the butter melts or the oil is hot, add the mushrooms. Cook, stirring for about 10 minutes, until the mushrooms begin to brown. Season with salt and pepper as they cook. Add the shallot and garlic and cook, stirring, for about a minute. Add the stock and bring the mixture just about to a boil. Turn off heat and allow this to cool for about 15 minutes. Use a blender or an immersion blender and blend the soup, in batches if using a blender, until the mushrooms are pureed. You can do this part up to 2 days in advance; refrigerate the soup in the meantime. When ready to serve, return to pot, warm as necessary, and add the cream. Heat thoroughly, but do not boil. Serve hot.

Roasted Sweet Potato and Carrot Soup

think I first found this recipe online. I am not really sure, because I subsequently lost it and had to recreate it. The house smells spicy and sweet when the vegetables are roasting with curry powder. The soup tastes as good as it smells.

1 lb (500 gm) sweet potatoes, peeled and cut into 1 inch chunks

slightly more than half a pound (300 gm) carrots, peeled and cut into 1 inch chunks

2 tbsp olive oil

1 tbsp curry powder

2 tbsp olive oil

2 large onions, chopped

2 cloves garlic, chopped

4 cups chicken broth

Heat oven to 375F. Toss sweet potatoes and carrots with olive oil, then curry powder. Place in a roasting pan and roast until caramelized and soft, about 25 minutes. When done, remove from oven and allow to cool a little. In a large sauce pan or pot, fry onions in olive oil for about 3 minutes, until soft. Add garlic and cook for another minute. Add chicken broth and simmer 10 to 15 minutes. Stir sweet potatoes and carrots into stock mixture. Puree either in batches in a blender, or with an immersion blender. Serve warm, and garnish with creme fraiche, sour cream or plain yogurt, as desired.

Chapter 3

Yeast and Quick Breads

When I feel intimidated by a bread recipe, I remind myself that people have been making bread for thousands of years, and usually in conditions far more rustic than my kitchen. Still, things can go wrong. The only times I have ruined a bread recipe in the past involved burning or undercooking, but in testing these recipes I over proofed two batches of bread in a row. Even if bread dough is underworked or over proofed, the end result will still be good with the appropriate amounts of butter or jam. In this section, the older recipes use a yeast proofing technique wherein you put the dry yeast in warm water and leave 10 minutes to bubble up. Some recipes skip this step altogether. I use either technique, depending on the recipe.

There are a few basic things to know about bread that are learned by experience. If you proof the yeast with warm water, use water that just feels warm on the inside of your wrist, the way you would test a baby's milk bottle. Let a few drops fall on your wrist; it should feel warm, not hot and not cool. If the recipe says knead the dough, place the dough on a floured surface and work it in a regular pulling motion for 8 to 10 minutes. I pull the bottom half of the dough toward me, folding it up and over. Think of the dough as the face of a clock: pull 6 o'clock over 12 o'clock and push down. Turn 3 'clock down to the 6 o'clock position and repeat. You will gradually get into the rhythm of kneading. You are done when the ball of dough feels smooth and you see bubbles stretching over the surface. Then do the window pane test: Take a small piece of dough and stretch it thin with your fingers. When the gluten is well activated, the dough will stretch thin and hold, so that you can see light through it. Finally, dough has finished proofing when you can poke it with two fingers and the dough sinks in a bit but does not bounce back. Use about a tablespoon of butter to grease two loaf pans; use about 2 tsp of oil to grease a bowl, if the recipe says to grease a bowl in which bread will rise.

Gloria's Raisin Oatmeal Bread

This is adapted from Marilyn Barbe's book, *Basically Bread*. I used this recipe to make sandwich loaves for several years. The whole grains and nuts create a dense bread that will not leave you hungry mid-afternoon. This recipe makes two loaves.

1/2 cup warm water

1 tsp sugar

2 tbsp yeast

1 3/4 cups boiling water

1 cup quick cooking oats

3 tsp salt

1/4 cup butter

1/2 cup honey

1/2 cup finely chopped walnuts (start with 3/4 cup walnut halves or pieces, and grind to a coarse meal in a food processor to make 1/2 cup)

1 cup raisins

3 cups whole wheat flour

2 cups white flour

In a measuring cup or bowl, pour 1/4 cup warm water. Add 1 tsp sugar but do not stir. Slowly sprinkle yeast into the water, making sure each particle gets wet. Do not stir. Wait 10 minutes.

In a large stand mixer bowl with a dough hook, or a bread bowl and a spoon, combine 2 cups boiling water, 1 cup oats, 3 tsp of salt, 1/4 cup butter, 1/2 cup honey, and 3 cups whole wheat flour, adding 1 cup at a time. Stir to cool, then add the yeast mixture. Add raisins, walnuts, and one cup white flour. Stir well. Dough will be sticky. Work the last cup of flour into the dough to make it stiff.

If making the dough manually, turn dough out onto lightly dusted work surface and knead 10 minutes. The dough may be sticky, but do not add too much flour. If using a stand mixer, leave running on low with dough hook for another 5 to 8 minutes. Turn out onto work surface and knead briefly, about 10 times.

Put dough in greased bowl, turn to grease the top, and allow to rise for 1 1/2 hours until doubled in size. Punch the dough down, knead briefly and cut in half. Shape into two loaves and place in greased loaf pans. Leave to rise for 30 minutes until doubled again. While bread is rising, preheat oven to 400F. Bake for 50 minutes. You may wish to cover the tops with foil during the last 10 minutes. Cool immediately on a wire rack.

Red River Bread

I like multigrain breads for all those health claims about whole grains, slow digestion, gut biome and the like. It has become easy to make a multigrain bread with products like Red River Cereal (available in Canada, or through online orders) or Bob's Red Mill 7 Grain cereal. This is also from Marilyn Barbe's *Basically Bread*. Makes 2 loaves.

2 1/2 cups warm water

1 tsp sugar

2 tbsp yeast

1/4 cup honey

2 tsp salt

1 cup Red River cereal OR Bob's Red Mill 7 Grain Cereal

1/4 cup melted butter

2 cups whole wheat flour

3 1/2 cups white flour

To proof the yeast, pour 2 1/2 cups warm tap water into bread bowl. Add sugar, do not stir. Add yeast, sprinkling carefully so that all particles get wet. Leave 10 minutes until yeast has foamed and puffed up. One at a time, add the honey, salt, Red River or 7 Grain cereal, 2 cups whole wheat flour and 1/4 cup melted butter, mixing well after each addition. Add the rest of the flour 1 cup at a time, stirring to blend with each addition.

Turn the dough out onto a well floured surface and knead 10 to 12 minutes until elastic. It should be less sticky than it was at first. Put the dough in a greased bowl, turn to grease the whole surface, and allow to rise until double in a draft free spot, about 1 1/2 hours. Shape into 2 loaves and place in well greased loaf pans. Leave to rise in a warm, draft-free place, until almost doubled, about 30 minutes.

While bread is rising, preheat oven to 400F. Bake for 30 minutes. Cool on a wire rack.

The Quickie Whole Wheat Bread

A friend wanted to start making bread, so she asked me to show her how. I picked this recipe from Marilyn Barbe's *Basically Bread*. All the essential steps, from proofing, rising, shaping and baking, were covered. She came over in the morning and this bread was baked and out of the oven by noon. Then we had lunch with some fresh bread. This makes two loaves.

2 1/4 cups warm water	1/4 cup melted butter
1 tsp sugar	4 cups whole wheat flour
1 1/2 tbsp yeast	2 cups white flour
1/4 cup molasses or honey	2 tsp salt

To proof the yeast, pour 2 1/2 cups warm tap water into bread bowl. Add sugar, but do not stir. Add yeast, sprinkling carefully so that all particles get wet. Leave 10 minutes until yeast has foamed and puffed up. To the bread bowl, one at a time add salt, molasses or honey, 1 cup whole wheat flour and 1/4 cup melted butter, mixing well after each addition. Add 3 cups whole wheat flour and 2 cups white flour, 1 cup at a time and mixing well with each addition to make a soft, sticky dough. Turn the dough out onto a well floured surface. Knead the dough until elastic, about 10 minutes.

Let the dough rest on the work surface for 10 minutes. Cut the dough in half. Weigh each half to be sure the loaves are of equal weight. Shape into loaves and place in well greased loaf pans. Allow the loaves to rise in a warm, draft free place until double, about 30 or 45 minutes.

While bread is rising, preheat oven to 400F. Bake for 30 minutes. Allow to cool on a wire rack.

Speedy No Knead Bread
(a French Boule)

This is Mark Bittman's recipe from The New York Times, reprinted in the Toronto Star on October 18, 2008, and is Bill's all time favourite bread. The recipe makes a single brown, rounded, crusty loaf. It is easy, reliable and good. The combination of a wet dough and a long proof results in a delicious bread. The parchment paper handles are a later modification I found in Cooks Illustrated.

3 cups bread flour (I use all purpose)	1 1/2 tsp salt
1 packet (1/4 ounce)(2 1/4 tsp) yeast	1 1/2 cups water
	Oil as needed

Combine flour, yeast and salt in a large bowl. Add water and stir until blended. You can use a stand mixer for this part. Mix until all the flour is incorporated. It will seem a wet, shaggy mess, but the prolonged rest will allow the flour to absorb the liquid. Remove the dough hook and leave the dough in the mixing bowl. Cover bowl with plastic wrap. Let dough rest about 4 hours or more at room temperature, about 70F, until doubled in size.

Lightly oil a work surface and turn out dough onto it. Turn dough over on itself once or twice. Cut 2 wide strips of parchment paper and lay them crosswise in an 8" fry pan with a lip. The ends should extend beyond the lip of the fry pan to form handles. Put the dough on top of the parchment paper, cover loosely with plastic wrap and allow to rest for 30 minutes more.

At the same time, place a large enameled cast iron lidded casserole or dutch oven pot with the lid on in the oven, and preheat oven to 450F. When the oven is fully heated and the dough is ready, carefully remove the pot from the oven. It will be very hot. Remove the lid. Pick up the dough by the parchment paper handles and place it in the heated pot. Leave the parchment paper in place and do not worry if the paper extends over the top of the pot.

Cover the pot with the lid and return to the oven. Bake for 30 minutes. Remove the lid and bake another 15 to 30 minutes, until loaf is beautifully browned. Cool on rack.

Egg Bread

This is another recipe that I have had for so long that I no longer remember the source. I think it is the first time I came across the trick of putting bread dough in a cold oven, then turning it on to increase the rise on the second proofing. If you braid the dough, the result will look like a traditional challah bread.

1 envelope (1/4 ounce)(2-1/4 tsp) yeast

1 tbsp sugar

1/2 cup warm water

1 beaten egg

1/2 cup melted lard

2 cups lukewarm water

1 1/2 tsp salt

1/2 cup sugar

8 cups all purpose flour

Dissolve one envelope yeast with 1 tablespoon of sugar and 1/2 half cup warm water. Melt 1/2 cup lard. Beat together 2 cups lukewarm water, one egg, and the lard. Stir in 1 1/2 tsp of salt and 1/2 cup sugar. Stir in proofed yeast mixture. Gradually add 8 cups of flour, one cup at a time to make a dough. Proof for 1 to 1 1/2 hours.

Punch down dough and form into three loaves. You can make three basic loaf shapes, or split each of the thirds into three ropes and braid them for three loaves in a traditional shape. Allow to rise for one hour or more.

Put the loaf pans in a cold oven and turn on to 400F. Bake for 15 minutes. Reduce heat to 375F and bake for 25 more minutes. Let cool.

One Pan Dinner Rolls

There is nothing quite like the smell of fresh bread in the air when friends come over for dinner. This recipe quickly produces a batch of pull-apart rolls, which were a thing at one time. I believe a coworker, Pat, gave me this recipe back in the mid 80's. Remember to have eggs and butter at room temperature before starting.

3 tbsp bulk yeast, or 3 packets yeast	2 eggs at room temperature
2 1/2 cups hot tap water	6 1/2 cups white all purpose flour
1/4 cup white sugar	1/2 cup whole wheat flour
1/2 cup butter at room temperature	1/2 cup powdered milk
2 tsp salt	

In a large mixing bowl, mix together yeast and sugar. In a second bowl, mix hot tap water and room temperature butter; stir until butter is almost melted. Pour the water/butter mix into the sugar and yeast bowl. Use a hand electric mixer at this stage. Add in 1 1/2 cups white flour, 1/2 cup whole wheat flour and salt. Mix well with the beaters. Stir in the powdered milk, then add 1 cup flour and the eggs, and mix for one minute. Add remaining flour, 1 cup at a time, beating after each addition. At some point the dough will become too stiff for the beaters. Continue mixing by hand at that point. When all the flour is incorporated, cover the bowl with a cloth and leave to rise in a warm, draft free spot. There is no need to grease the bowl. Allow dough to rise until double, about 1 1/2 hours, or 1 hour in a slightly warmed oven.

Melt a few tablespoons butter and set aside with a pastry brush. When the dough has risen, punch down and turn out on to a lightly floured surface. Shape 2" round rolls and brush sides with melted butter. This will keep the rolls separate and prevent them from rising together into one large lump. Arrange the rolls in a greased tin or low sided casserole. This may take two pans. Cover the rolls and let them rise for 1/2 hour. Preheat oven to 400F. Bake for 15 to 25 minutes until lightly browned.

Alternatively, once the rolls are formed and in the pan, place them in the cold oven and let them rise for 20 minutes. After 20 minutes has passed, turn the oven on to 400F. The rolls will continue to rise while the oven heats. Bake for 15 to 25 minutes until lightly browned. Turn the pan out onto a serving dish; the rolls are pulled apart at the table.

Poppy Seed Bread

Throughout this book, there are recipes I have found and made over the years just because Bill likes them. When Bill was an undergraduate at Brock University, he loved the Poppy Seed Roll at Jane's Bakery. The bakery is not there anymore, but this recipe comes close.

Dough:

- 1 tsp sugar
- 1/4 cup lukewarm water
- 1 tbsp active dry yeast (or 1 envelope active dry yeast)
- 1/2 cup milk, scalded and cooled
- 1/2 cup sifted flour
- 1/4 cup unsalted butter, softened
- 1/3 cup sugar
- 3 eggs
- 1/4 tsp salt
- 1/2 tsp vanilla
- 1 tsp grated lemon rind
- 3 cups sifted all-purpose flour

Filling:

- 8 ounces (225 gm) poppy seeds, finely ground (use a coffee or spice grinder)
- 1 tbsp grated lemon rind
- 1 tbsp lemon juice
- 1 tbsp orange juice
- 1/2 cup honey

To make the filling, combine ingredients and blend to a fine paste.

To make the bread, dissolve 1 tsp sugar in the water and sprinkle the yeast over the water. Allow to proof for 5 minutes. Beat in the 1/2 cup flour, softened butter, 1/3 cup sugar, 2 eggs and salt. Stir in the vanilla, lemon rind and remaining 3 cups flour. Mix thoroughly then knead for 10 minutes. The dough will be soft. Allow to rise twice.

On the last rise, punch down and roll out into a rectangle. Beat the egg white from the last egg and brush on the dough. Spread the filling on the dough and roll up on the long axis. Let rise until double.

While rising, preheat oven to 350F. Brush the roll with the beaten yolk of the egg and put in oven for 10 minutes. Reduce heat to 300F and cook for 50 more minutes.

Scottish Scones

When I was in high school, in the village of Beloeil, Quebec, I made friends with a new girl at school named Shelley. A couple of years later she was chatting with my grandfather Jordan when they discovered her grandfather was his first cousin, and they had both grown up on the Saskatchewan prairies. This made Shelley and I third cousins. Back to the scones. This is an original Scottish recipe from Shelley's mother. It had been in her family for quite a long time. This recipe is transcribed just as Shelley's mother gave it to me without any modifications. I had thought to try and quantify "a pinch of salt" and "enough milk to make a paste", but I hate to lose the ambience of the recipe. Give this recipe a try if you are comfortable enough with baking to wing it a little.

Makes 9 2 1/2 inch wide scones

2 cups flour	1/4 cup shortening
1 tsp baking soda	2 eggs
1 tsp cream of tartar	1/2 cup raisins or currants
Pinch of salt	enough milk to make a paste (start with 1/4 cup milk and increase a few tablespoons at a time to bring dough together)
3/4 cup white sugar	
1/4 cup butter	

Preheat oven to 425F.

Sift flour, baking soda, cream of tartar, salt and sugar together. Cut in the butter and shortening. Add eggs, milk, raisins and blend. The dough must not be too soft, but not too tough. Pat the dough into 1 inch thick rounds and place on a greased baking sheet. Bake for 15 to 18 minutes until golden brown. Split, butter and eat with strawberry jam while warm.

Blueberry Oat Bran Scones

This scone is rich with butter and eggs, and has become a favourite. I have at times substituted chopped fresh strawberries, with good results. If you use strawberries, use early ones before they become heavy with juice. This will limit the juice from running into the scone and turning it red.

- 1 1/2 cups oat bran
- 1 1/2 cups flour
- 1/3 cup brown sugar
- 2 tsp baking powder
- 1 tsp cream of tartar
- 1/2 cup butter

- 2 eggs
- 1/3 cup yogurt
- a small amount of milk (see directions, below)
- 1 tsp vanilla
- 1 1/2 cups blueberries, fresh or frozen OR fresh early strawberries, chopped to blueberry size

Preheat oven to 400F. Lightly grease a baking sheet. Blend together oat bran, flour, sugar, baking powder and cream of tartar. Cut in butter until mixture is crumbly. In a measuring cup, mix together eggs, yogurt and vanilla. Add enough milk to bring the egg/yogurt mix to 1/2 cup of liquid. Add to dry ingredients and mix well after each addition. Stir into dry ingredients. The dough will be stiff. Fold in blueberries. Shape into an 8" circle on the baking sheet. Mark 8 wedges without cutting through the dough. Bake for 20 to 25 minutes.

Scottish Oat Scones with Walnuts

I took a weekend trip recently and decided to bring a breakfast scone to my hosts. I wanted something with a little more substance than my usual scone. I ended up with a recipe from the Quaker Oats website, but modified it to be less sweet. This scone is rich and buttery, and the walnuts add a pleasant nutty dimension.

1 1/2 cups flour

1 cup old fashioned long cooking oats

1/4 cup granulated sugar

1 tbsp baking powder

1/4 tsp salt

1/2 cup (8 tbsp or 1 stick) unsalted cold butter, cut in pieces

1/2 cup chopped walnuts

1/3 cup milk

1 egg, lightly beaten

Preheat oven to 400F. Lightly grease a baking sheet. In a large bowl, combine flour, oats, sugar, baking powder and salt. Cut in butter using a pastry blender or two knives until the mixture resembles coarse crumbs. Stir in the walnuts. In a separate bowl, beat together the milk and egg. Add to dry ingredients all at once, and blend just until dry ingredients are moistened.

Turn out onto a lightly floured surface; there may be crumbs. Knead together 8 or 10 times. Roll or pat dough out to an 8 inch circle, about 1/2 inch thick. Score the top with a knife to mark 8 wedges. Bake 18 to 20 minutes until light golden brown.

Whole Wheat Biscuits

To my mind, the purpose of biscuits is to cover a casserole of thick chicken or beef stew. Voila, pot pie. This recipe is lightly adapted from Edna Staebler's *Schmecks Appeal*. The recipe originally called for just all purpose flour. I substituted one cup whole wheat cake and pastry flour for the all purpose flour for a heartier taste on the pie.

1 cup all purpose white flour

1 cup whole wheat cake and pastry flour

1 tsp baking powder

1 tsp baking soda

1/4 tsp salt

1/3 cup shortening

2/3 cup milk soured with 1 tbsp lemon juice

Put 1 tbsp lemon juice in a cup measure and add enough milk to make 2/3 cup. Let it sit to sour about 10 minutes. Place the flours, baking soda, baking powder and salt in a food processor and run briefly to mix. Cut cold shortening into pieces and place in the flour mixture. Process for a few seconds, until mixture has the consistency of sand with a few small lumps. Pour soured milk into flour mixture and process very briefly, or pulse, until mixture starts to hold together. Turn out onto floured surface and knead briefly until dough holds together in a ball.

To make a topping for a chicken pot pie, roll dough out into a sheet and cut to fit top of casserole. Lay over filling and make a few slashes in the top to allow steam to escape. Bake at 425F until golden.

For biscuits, roll dough out to 1/2 inch thickness. Cut out biscuits, lay on nonstick sheet pan, and bake at 425F for 20 to 25 minutes, until golden.

Irish Soda Bread

From McCall's Cookbook 1963. I first made this when I was very young, and had not yet tried to make a yeasted bread. This is a quick way to get a fresh loaf of bread on the table. I made it again recently when my friend, Wendy, came for a visit. She grew up in England in the 60's and pronounced this version completely authentic in density, taste and crumb. A soda bread has a bit of bite in the taste, due to the soda, so we ate slices of it with local cheese and rhubarb chutney. It all balanced very well with a chilled pinot grigio on a shady front porch.

4 cups sifted all purpose flour

1 tbsp baking soda

1 tbsp sugar

2 1/2 tsp salt

1/4 tsp cream of tartar

1 1/2 cups buttermilk

1 tbsp butter, melted

Preheat oven to 375F. Grease a large cookie sheet well. In large bowl, combine flour with soda, sugar, salt and cream of tartar. Add buttermilk and stir with a fork just until dry ingredients are moistened. Turn out dough onto lightly floured board. Knead about one minute until smooth. Shape dough into a ball. Place on cookie sheet and form into a 7 inch circle.

With knife, make slices one quarter inch deep in the shape of a cross, making quarters. Bake 30 to 40 minutes until top is golden brown, and loaf sounds hollow when tapped. Brush top with melted butter. Cool completely.

Bannock

This recipe is from Carol Ferguson's *Canadian Living Cookbook* (1987). I include it here as a nod to family. "Bannock" was my mother's nickname when she was a child living in Saskatchewan, because she tanned so brown in the summer. This bread is similar to a scone. It was a staple with First Nations and settlers, and was often baked over an open fire. This recipe is easily varied, depending on what flours and fats are available.

3 cups all purpose flour (or a mixture of flours)

2 tbsp baking powder

1 tbsp granulated sugar

1 tsp salt

1/2 cup lard (or butter)

1 cup water (or milk, for a richer dough)

Preheat oven to 425F. Mix together flour, baking powder, sugar and salt. Cut in (or rub in with fingers) lard to a fine consistency. Gradually add enough water or milk to make a soft dough. Form into a ball and press into a circle 1 inch thick. Place in a cast iron pan, on a baking sheet, or on a hot flat rock fireside. Bake for about 25 minutes, until lightly browned. Cut in wedges and serve with butter.

Chapter 4

Vegetarian and Mostly Meatless Dishes

'Vegetarian' can cover a real range of dishes, with different choices in meatless, dairy free or vegan approaches. Some of the recipes here have a small amount of meat, usually bacon, for flavour. I admit that the first time I ate lentils I thought I had a mouthful of mud. I hated the texture and taste. It was not until I tried Chef Michael Smith's recipe for lentils with bacon and vegetables that I really liked them.

Lentils and Bacon

I started making this to take to work for lunch. It was inexpensive, tasty and I could make a week's worth in one easy go. I did not always have fresh tarragon, so I left it out or substituted 1/2 tsp dried tarragon. Chef Michael Smith developed this recipe, and I found it on the Canadian Lentil Farmers website. Chef Smith did a series of cooking videos for the Canadian Lentil Farmers. He said, "The best thing about lentils is bacon!".

8 slices of bacon, thinly sliced

A big splash of water

1 large onion, minced

2 stalks of celery, chopped

2 carrots, peeled and thinly sliced

4 cloves of garlic, thinly sliced

1 cup of green lentils

3 cups of water

1/2 teaspoon of salt

1 bay leaf

1 teaspoon of any vinegar or the juice of half a lemon

1 tablespoon of fresh tarragon, chopped

In a large saucepan over medium high heat, toss in the bacon then pour in enough water to just barely cover it. Stir frequently with a wooden spoon. As the water simmers, the bacon will begin to cook. Then as the water evaporates the bacon will render, releasing its fat, and will crisp as the fat left behind heats past the boiling point of water into the flavour zone. Stir and be patient; it is worth getting every piece evenly crisped, about five or six minutes. If you like, pour off half of the bacon drippings.

Toss in the carrots, onions, celery, and garlic and continue cooking, stirring until the veggies are heated through and their flavour brightens, two to three minutes.

Stir in the lentils, water, salt, and bay leaf. Bring everything to a full boil then lower the heat, adjusting it so the liquid is barely simmering. Simmer uncovered until the lentils are tender and most of the water has been absorbed, about 20 minutes or so. Stir in the lemon juice and tarragon. Remove bay leaf before serving.

Boursin Potatoes

This brilliant dish is adapted slightly from the Boursin website. The house smells wonderful when it is baking. It is easy to make, the finished product looks great, and it tastes as good as it smells. This is also a recipe that will tolerate some minor substitutions. I have made it with gold flesh potatoes, half and half cream (10% butterfat) and left out the chives or parsley.

3 lbs red potatoes, unpeeled

salt and pepper

1 pint (2 cup, 16 oz) heavy cream

1 (5 ounce) package Boursin cheese with garlic and chives

chives or parsley, chopped

Preheat oven to 350F. Slice potatoes into quarter inch rounds and toss with salt and pepper. Slowly heat cream and cheese together until cheese is thoroughly melted. In a deep oiled or greased casserole dish layer half the potatoes. Cover with half the cream mixture. Repeat. Cover and bake in oven for one hour. Sprinkle top with chives or parsley and serve.

Chickpea and Sweet Potato Curry

If the dinner crowd is mixed vegetarian and omnivore, this makes a good addition to the table. The flavours are warm and spicy, and it can be made with basic things on hand like a can of chickpeas, a can of coconut milk, curry powder and sweet potatoes. I have made this without the chili, which is my favourite.

2 tbsp canola oil

1 small yellow onion, chopped

2 garlic cloves, finely chopped

1 tbsp. chopped fresh ginger

1 Thai or jalapeño chili, seeded and finely chopped

1 tbsp. curry powder

Salt and freshly ground pepper, to taste

1 large sweet potato, peeled and cut into 1/2-inch cubes

1 can (15 oz.) chickpeas, drained and rinsed

1 can (14 fl. oz.) coconut milk, well shaken

1 cup water

1/2 cup frozen peas

1/2 cup canned diced tomatoes, drained

Steamed basmati rice for serving (optional)

In a heavy bottomed saucepan over medium to low heat, warm the oil. Add the onion, garlic, ginger and chili and cook, stirring occasionally, until the onion is translucent, about 4 minutes. Stir in the curry powder and cook, stirring constantly, until fragrant, about 30 seconds. Season with salt and pepper.

Add the sweet potato, chickpeas, coconut milk and water to the pan. Raise the heat to medium high, bring just to a boil, reduce the heat and simmer, uncovered, until the sweet potato is tender, about 10 minutes. Add the peas and tomatoes and cook until heated through. Serve in bowls over steamed rice, if desired. Serves 4.

Szechuan Dan Dan Noodles

Spicy peanut sauce on noodles just has to be good, but it is not a light dish. Finding the Szechuan peppercorns can be an arduous task, but the flavour they bring to the dish, even in such a small amount, is absolutely worth it. One package of Szechuan peppercorns will last a long, long time.

Sauce:

- 1/2 cup +2 tbsp chunky peanut butter
- 1/4 tsp red pepper
- 3 or 4 tbsp minced green onion
- 3 tbsp soy sauce
- 2 tbsp vinegar

- 1 to 2 tsp of crushed garlic
- 1 tsp sugar (optional)
- 1/4 tsp crushed Szechuan peppercorns
- up to 1/4 cup warm water as needed

Noodles:

- 1 pound rice noodles

- 1 box of frozen spinach, thawed and drained

Blend the sauce ingredients together in a sauce pan and warm, adding a little water if needed to thin to a sauce-like consistency. I have added up to 1/4 cup or more of warm water. Warm gently over a low heat. Cook noodles according to package directions and drain. Pour the sauce over the noodles. Toss with spinach and serve.

Meatless Loaf

Try not to think of this in comparison to meatloaf; it is an interesting dish all on its own. This recipe is unchanged from the one given to me decades ago by Barb. Judith from the Test Kitchen Committee used 3 eggs and loved the result. She said it was not unlike a good turkey stuffing, and it was tasty the next day served cold with salad."

1 onion finely chopped

2 tbsp butter

1 tbsp lemon juice

2 cups of bread or cracker crumbs

1 cup chopped walnuts

1 cup grated cheddar cheese

2 or 3 beaten eggs

1 1/3 cup yogurt, or milk and yogurt together

1/2 tsp each dried marjoram and savory

a dash of Worcestershire sauce

Preheat oven to 375F. Melt butter in pan and sauté onions until transparent. Mix crumbs, nuts and cheese together with onions. In a separate bowl, beat eggs, lemon juice and yogurt, with marjoram, savory and Worcestershire sauce and then mix thoroughly with onion walnut mixture. Place in greased loaf pan and place that in a shallow pan of water. Bake for 40 to 60 minutes and serve with mushroom or chili sauce.

Rice Mexican Style

I constantly play with recipes, changing ingredients to suit what I like or have on hand. The first time I realized the importance of producing a recipe exactly as written was this dish, from a book called Mexican Cookery (De La Rosa and De Fernandez, 1979). Our friend Gord, who had lived and worked in southern California, sat in the kitchen eating this. I saw him look up, smile and say, "This is exactly how she made it". I was happy that I had not altered the dish in any way.

1 1/4 quarter cups long grain rice

4 tablespoons lard or oil

8 ounces tomatoes, peeled, seeded and puréed

1 tbsp minced onion

1 cup cold water

1/2 tsp salt

8 ounces green peas, shelled

2 cups hot chicken broth

Soak rice in hot water to cover for 15 minutes. Wash in several changes of cold water until the water runs clear, then drain in a sieve. Heat the lard or oil in a pan and fry rice, stirring constantly until the rice is opaque. Drain excess lard or oi with a spoon. Add tomato purée and onion to the rice and cook over high heat, stirring until rice is almost dry. Add the cold water, salt and peas, and simmer uncovered until the rice is almost dry again. Add the hot broth. Cover the pot, and simmer until the rice is dry and the grains have separated, 25 for 30 minutes.

Quiche Lorraine

Redbook magazine used to feature booklets of recipes in a themed monthly supplement back in the 60's. This recipe came from the Switzerland installment. I first tried it while living in what was known as the Student Ghetto near McGill University when I was an undergraduate. It is nutty and delicious, and best when made with a good Emmentaler cheese.

1 9 inch pie shell, unbaked

6 ounces grated or diced Swiss cheese (Emmentaler is preferred)

8 slices crumbled crisp bacon

3 eggs

1 cup heavy cream (I use 10%, also called Half and Half)

1/2 cup milk

1/2 tsp salt

1/4 tsp pepper

1/4 tsp paprika

1/2 tsp dry mustard

Preheat oven to 375F. Place the Swiss cheese in the pie shell. Crumble bacon on top. Beat together eggs, cream, milk and seasonings. Pour the milk and egg mixture over the cheese. Bake for 45 minutes, until puffed and golden.

Tortellini Casserole

This is from a Milk Calendar, which was published annually with the newspaper, back in the days of print newspapers, and probably before 1995. As I look at it now, this recipe is a variation of macaroni and cheese casseroles from the 60's. I keep frozen tortellini on hand as a staple in the larder.

Sauce:

1/4 cup butter

2 cloves garlic, finely chopped

1 small onion, finely chopped

1/4 cup all purpose flour

2 cups milk

1 cup pureed canned tomatoes or

tomato sauce

1 tbsp tomato paste

1/2 tsp each dried thyme, basil and oregano

1 tsp salt

1/2 tsp pepper

Filling:

1 lb cheese tortellini

1 bunch fresh broccoli, trimmed and cut into chunks

2 cups grated cheddar cheese

1/2 cup grated Parmesan

To make the sauce, melt butter in sauce pan and sauté onion and garlic. Stir in the flour to make a roux. When it has cooked 3 or 4 minutes (do not brown), stir in the milk and bring to a boil. Add tomatoes, tomato paste, herbs, sat and pepper. Cook 5 minutes.

Meanwhile, preheat oven to 350F. In a large pot of boiling salted water, cook tortellini for 5 minutes. Then add broccoli to the boiling water and cook 5 minutes more. Drain. In a large bowl, stir together tortellini, broccoli and sauce. Stir in cheddar cheese. Pour into a greased casserole and sprinkle Parmesan over top. Bake for 30 minutes, until hot and lightly browned.

Mediterranean Eggplant Casserole

I first made this recipe up in the early 90's when I was looking for something very quick to pull together for a dinner party. I last served this dish for a couple who came to dinner; he was a vegetarian, she was an omnivore. I made this, as well as a pan of Balsamic Chicken and Peppers (see Chapter 6 Poultry), both of which are very straightforward to assemble and go straight into the oven.

This makes two 9" x 13" casseroles. There is no need to fry mushrooms, eggplant or onions ahead of time; everything cooks slowly in the sauce. If you go the route of using a pre-made sauce instead of cooking your own, this dish goes together even quicker.

Preheat oven to 325F. Grease two 9"x13" pans.

Sauce: (or use 2 to 3 jars of a good quality tomato sauce)

4 large (798 ml) tins diced tomatoes	1 small tin tomato paste
2 – 3 tbsp olive oil	1 tsp salt
4 large or 6 medium garlic cloves, chopped	1/2 tsp black pepper
	3 tbsp basil pesto

Vegetables:

3 eggplants, peeled and sliced about 1/4 inch thick	2 large red onions, sliced 1/4 inch thick
1 1/2 lb cremini mushrooms, sliced 1/4 to 1/2 inch thick.	2 lb mozzarella, shredded

First, make the tomato sauce. If you are short on time, skip this step and open 2 or more jars of your favourite tomato sauce. To make the sauce, sauté the garlic in the olive oil until fragrant but do not allow to brown. Stir in tinned tomatoes, tomato paste, pesto, salt and pepper and cook until thickened.

To assemble the casseroles, have the sauce and sliced vegetables set out. Layer the oiled casseroles with eggplant, onions, mushrooms, sauce and cheese in that order, repeating for a total of two layers in each pan. I recommend putting the pans on cookie sheets in case the sauce overflows over during baking. Bake for 50 to 60 minutes, until top is browned and vegetables are tender.

Red Cabbage with Apple and Quince

It all started with an episode of Kew Garden on BBC. A cheerful presenter, Kate Humble, and a chef, Raymond Blanc, enthused over the flavours of quince. They went on at length about the beauty and flavour of their quince jelly. I finally tracked some quince jelly down in a supermarket under the French name of Gelee de Coings, made by Gelee Bonne Maman. I used it as a glaze on an apple tart, and then this dish. This basic recipe came from a now-forgotten website. I substituted the quince jelly for sugar for a subtler flavour.

4 cups shredded red cabbage

1 small white onion, chopped

1 tbsp oil

1 tbsp maple syrup

1/2 tsp salt

1 tsp lemon juice

1 medium tart apple, chopped

4 tbsp quince jelly (the only brand I have been able to find in the supermarket is Gelee Bonne Maman Coings, which is French for quince jelly)

Mix all ingredients except apple and quince jelly in a heavy saucepan or dutch oven. Cook over medium heat until cabbage is lightly cooked. Stir in apple and cook 10 to 15 minutes longer. Stir in jelly, heat and serve.

Chapter 5

Vegetables and Salads

ike many born in the 50's and 60's, I grew up on iceberg lettuce salad, and it took me a long time to develop any skill with vegetables and salads. As a consequence, the recipes I do like to make have a lot of flavour and interest.

Tomato Gruyere Tart

I made this when all of the tomatoes in the garden were ripening at once. I wanted to do something special with them to reflect how wonderful it is to have fresh red tomatoes. This dish is easy and beautiful, and the combination of Gruyere and Dijon is a knockout.

1/2 package (or one sheet) frozen puff pastry, thawed

1 tbsp Dijon mustard

1 shallot, minced

1 cup (or 4 oz) shredded Gruyere cheese

1 lb fresh ripe tomatoes.

1/4 tsp dried thyme OR 1/2 tsp fresh thyme leaves

salt and freshly ground pepper

Preheat oven to 375F. Roll out puff pastry to 8" x 15" rectangle. Place on parchment paper on baking sheet. Leaving a 1" border, spread Dijon mustard over pastry. Sprinkle the shallots, then the cheese, over the mustard. Slice the tomatoes thinly (about 1/8 inch) and layer over cheese. Sprinkle thyme, salt and pepper as desired, over the top. Bake until the pastry is puffed and brown, about 25 minutes. Cut into slices and serve warm.

Broiled Fennel with Lime and Parmesan

It is easy to find rich vegetable dishes, but a simple dish can be more elusive. Once in a while, I come across a truly great recipe like this one from *Cooking Thin with Chef Kathleen* (2002). This method of cooking firm green vegetables at high heat for a light char also works very well with asparagus, broccolini and even bok choy. The result is slightly sweet and smoky.

3 tbsp olive oil

2 large fennel bulbs, trimmed top and bottom, cut length wise into one quarter inch slices

salt and pepper

Juice of 2 limes

6 tablespoons grated Parmesan cheese

Preheat broiler. Pour about 1 1/2 tablespoons olive oil onto each of two cookie sheets. Place fennel in a single layer on cookie sheets. Turn fennel slices over to coat both sides with oil. Use a pastry brush or your fingers if needed. Season with salt and pepper and squeeze the juice of one lime over the slices. Broil for five minutes, turn over, top with Parmesan and put back under broiler for 1 1/2 to 3 minutes. Just before serving, squeeze the juice from the second lime over the fennel slices.

Mushrooms Parmentier

We invited friends over for dinner on the weekend, and mushrooms were on sale at the supermarket. I brought them home and found this recipe from Laura Calder, originally on a website but ultimately from her book, *French Food at Home.* This is a showstopping dish; it takes some time but it is worth it. I return to it again and again.

Mushrooms:

2 lb mushrooms (white button, cremini or mixture of both)

3 tbsp butter

2 tbsp olive oil, or more as needed

1 large red onion, chopped

3 cloves garlic

a handful of fresh thyme leaves, chopped

1/2 cup red wine

1/2 cup mushroom stock (I use Better then Bouillon Mushroom Base) or water

salt and peppercorns

1 tbsp flour

a handful of chopped parsley

Potato Topping:

6 medium yellow flesh potatoes such as Yukon Gold, peeled

2 to 4 tbsp butter

1/4 cup milk

salt and pepper

4 oz Comte or Gruyere cheese, cut into very fine dice

2 tbsp Parmesan cheese

Preheat the oven to 425F. Clean and quarter the mushrooms. Sauté mushrooms in 2 tbsp butter and 1 tbsp olive oil just until golden. Remove from pan. Heat another tbsp of oil, or more if needed, and sauté the onion until soft. Add the garlic and cook one minute more. Deglaze the pan with the wine and reduce to no more than a spoonful. Add the stock, thyme and mushrooms, and salt and pepper to taste. Cook until the stock has reduced by half. Knead the flour together with the last tablespoon of butter and stir it in. Cook until the liquid has thickened to a sauce (only a few minutes). Stir in the parsley. Spoon into an oiled or greased casserole dish.

Cook the potatoes until very tender, preferably by steaming. Mash with the butter and milk until very smooth. Add more milk if needed. Season with salt and pepper if desired. Stir diced cheese through. Drop by spoonfuls over the mushrooms and spread to cover. Sprinkle Parmesan over. Bake until bubbling hot and golden on top, about 15 minutes.

51

Greek Salad with Tortellini

When my husband and I were at our busiest, both working full time and often tired and out of ideas for dinner, we bought a lot of pre-made salads at the supermarket. Most often it was Greek salad, with sliced black olives that always reminded me of black rubber washers. I started making this salad on weekends, when I had some time set aside to work in the kitchen. With the tortellini added, and no mayonnaise or eggs, this salad is perfect for a summer buffet, group dinner or potluck.

Salad:

1 (20 ounce) package refrigerated or frozen cheese tortellini

1 1/2 cups grape tomatoes, cut in half

1 large cucumber, chopped

1 cup kalamata olives, pit removed and chopped

1/2 red onion, chopped

3/4 cup crumbled feta cheese

Dressing:

1/4 cup extra virgin olive oil

3 tbsp red wine vinegar

1 clove garlic, minced

1/2 tsp dried oregano

Salt and pepper, to taste

Bring a large pot of salted water to a boil. Cook the tortellini according to the package directions. Drain the tortellini, rinse with cold water and drain again. Place the tortellini in a large bowl. Add the tomatoes, cucumber, olives, red onion, and feta cheese. In a small bowl, whisk together the olive oil, vinegar, garlic, oregano, salt, and pepper. Pour the dressing over the salad and stir until salad is well coated. Serve immediately or place in the refrigerator for up to 3 days.

Red Thing, Green Thing Salad

had told my husband I didn't think I was very good at making salads. Bill showed me this how-to video online, from Natasha's Kitchen website. As I watched it over his shoulder, I started saying "Green thing, red thing, green thing, red thing, got it" out loud as a mnemonic. The salad is fast, tasty and attractive.

1 cucumber, English or basic, peeled and sliced

2 medium ripe tomatoes, chopped

2 ripe avocados, peeled, pitted and sliced

1/2 medium red onion, sliced in rings

2 to 3 tbsp lemon juice, or juice of half a lemon

1/2 bunch fresh coriander, chopped.

1/2 to 1 tsp coarse salt and a few grinds of fresh black pepper

extra virgin olive oil, about 1/3 cup

Layer the cucumber, tomato, avocado and red onion in that order in a salad bowl. Next, sprinkle the lemon juice over top. Add salt and pepper to taste. Place the coriander on top. Pour oil over everything. Toss just before serving.

Cold Soba Noodle Salad

Like the Tortellini Salad, this can be made ahead and chilled in the refrigerator until ready to go. Like ice cream, cold noodle dishes need strong flavours to come through the coolness of the ingredients. Nut flavours are really nice in this format; see Szechuan Noodles Dan Dan in Chapter 4, for example. This recipe is good for a summer buffet.

Sesame Lime Ginger Dressing:

Juice of half a lime (full lime if the lime is small or less juicy)

1 tbsp minced ginger

1 tsp sesame oil, plus more for coating noodles

1 1/2 tbsp soy sauce

1 tbsp rice vinegar

1 1/2 tbsp maple syrup

2 tsp Asian chili sauce (sambal oelek) or sriracha or other hot sauce to taste

Noodle Salad:

7 to 8 oz soba noodles

1 red bell pepper, thinly sliced

1 cup sliced carrots

6 or 7 green onions (green parts chopped and divided)

1 zucchini or cucumber, thinly sliced

Sesame seeds , green onion, cilantro/mint (optional), crushed roasted peanuts or cashews (optional) for garnish

Mix the dressing ingredients in a bowl. Taste and adjust sweet, heat and sour elements to your liking. Chill for 15 minutes. Cook the noodles according to instructions on the package. Drain and rinse with cold water. Put the noodles in a large bowl, add a teaspoon of sesame oil and toss to coat. Add the vegetables (pepper, carrots, zucchini or cucumber) and half of the green onions to the bowl. Add the dressing to the bowl and toss well. Taste and adjust. Add salt or soy sauce for saltier flavour, a bit more maple syrup if needed, lime or vinegar for sour. Garnish as you like or have on hand: green onions, crushed nuts, cilantro or mint and sesame seeds. Chill and serve.

Oil and Vinegar Salad Dressing

A vinaigrette dressing is simply 2 or 3 parts oil to one part vinegar, and flavourings as desired. Salt and pepper, chopped garlic and flavoured oil are common additions. Balsamic vinegar and olive oil are already strongly flavoured, and need nothing else. Since this particular salad dressing has only two ingredients, go for the best quality you can find.

Extra virgin olive oil (the oil should have a green tinge and appear thicker than peanut oil)

Balsamic vinegar (be sure the label carries a "DOP" stamp for authenticity)

Combine the above in a 3 to 1 ratio- for example, 1/3 cup balsamic vinegar, 1 cup olive oil. When making a larger quantity, pour them both into a jar with a good stopper or lid, and shake well before using. For a single salad, try using 1 tablespoon of balsamic vinegar and 3 tablespoons oil at a time; whisk together and use immediately.

Caesar Salad Dressing

It seems reasonable that a creamy salad dressing could start with a mayonnaise base. This one is pretty easy to make, and has a great garlic flavour. The recipe is from Jenn Segal's *Once Upon A Chef.* It keeps for about a week in the fridge.

2 small garlic cloves, minced

1 tsp anchovy paste (buy it by the tube; I found it at the fish counter in the supermarket)

2 tbsp lemon juice

1 tsp Dijon mustard

1 tsp Worcestershire sauce

1 cup good quality mayonnaise

1/2 cup freshly grated Parmigiano-Reggiano

1/4 tsp salt

1/4 tsp freshly ground pepper

Whisk cloves, anchovy paste, lemon juice, mustard and Worcestershire sauce together in a medium bowl. Then whisk in mayonnaise and cheese. Taste and add salt and pepper to taste.

Oven Fried Potatoes

I t's a simple method, and I have seen it made with ovens set to 400F or 425F. You can add in sliced kielbasa, whole garlic sausage, or herbs.

4 to 5 potatoes, peeled and cut into wedges

salt

1 tbsp oil

Preheat oven to 375F.

Toss potatoes in oil, lay out in a single layer on a baking sheet. Sprinkle with salt. If using, add in sausage. Roast for 45 minutes, or until browned, and serve.

Chapter 6

Poultry

In 2018 I started buying local, organic, free run chickens. These chickens, roasted whole, smelled and tasted the way Bill and I remember chicken from our childhood. We were both amazed at the difference in flavour, compared to supermarket chicken. The local organic chicken costs a good deal more, but if I am going to roast a chicken these days, it is the way I'll go.

Uncle Al's Glazed Turkey

Uncle Al was a good cook, and his stuffed turkey was always juicy and tasty. He told me many years ago how he made his special turkey, after some entreating on my part. He did not measure with any rigour, and when I make this, neither do I.

1 large turkey, 15 to 18 pounds   1/3 cup brown sugar, packed

1/3 cup softened butter   1 - 2 tbsp dry mustard

Preheat the oven to 425F. Stuff the turkey with your favourite dressing. Sew up the cavity and truss the legs. Place the turkey in a pan with a roasting rack and wipe dry with paper towels.

Mix together the butter, brown sugar and dry mustard, blending everything to a paste. Smear all over turkey. If the butter is cold, you can melt it in the microwave, stir in the brown sugar and dry mustard, then brush on the turkey with a pastry brush. Place the turkey in the oven and bake for 10 minutes or so to set the glaze. Turn the heat down to 325F and cook for 20 minutes per pound. Toward the end of cooking, place an aluminum foil tent over the turkey to prevent burning. Check for doneness with a meat thermometer in the thickest part of the thigh; it should be 165F. I also grab the tip of the drumstick and wiggle it; if it moves very easily, it is done. An unstuffed turkey will cook faster than a stuffed turkey. This recipe will result in a dark brown glaze over the whole bird. Remove from the oven and let rest 20 to 30 minutes before carving.

Basic Onion Sage Stuffing

This is my default stuffing recipe and I love the aroma. This will stuff a turkey in the 15 to 18 pound range.

3 tbsp unsalted butter

1 large or 2 medium yellow onions, chopped

1 tsp each dried thyme and sage

1/2 tsp salt and 1/4 tsp pepper

6 cups stale bread cubes

Place the bread cubes in a large bowl. Melt the butter in a sauté pan and add onions, thyme and sage. Cook the onions until transparent. Pour this over the bread crumbs, and add salt and pepper to taste. Stuff the turkey, including the neck cavity, and close one cavity with the neck skin flap, and one by crossing the turkey legs and putting them through the skin loop at the neck.

B'stilla

This is an all day, multiple step recipe. It calls for so much time that I keep it aside as a very special occasion dish. I first had this at Lucy and Kim's place; Lucy had spent much of the day preparing it. When we walked in the front door of their house the aroma was wonderful. It is time consuming, complicated and special.

2 lb chicken legs

2 cups water

1/4 cup unsalted butter

1/2 cup chopped fresh parsley

2 large onions, chopped medium

1/4 tsp cinnamon

1/4 tsp saffron

1/4 tsp dry ginger

1/2 ground black pepper

1/4 tsp turmeric

pinch of salt (about 1/8 tsp)

1/4 cup vegetable oil (for frying almonds)

1/4 cup whole blanched onions

1/4 cup powdered sugar (I have omitted this with no problem)

1 tsp cinnamon

1/4 cup unsalted butter, melted

6 eggs, well beaten

12 sheets phyllo pastry

Combine first 11 ingredients (chicken, water, butter, parsley, onions, cinnamon, saffron, ginger, pepper, turmeric and salt) in a pot. Cover and bring to a boil. Simmer for an hour, stirring occasionally. Fry the almonds, let them cool, and chop them in a food processor. Add sugar, (if using) cinnamon and butter.

Take the chicken mixture off the heat and allow to cool. Remove the chicken legs from the broth, let cool and remove meat from the bones. Shred the meat and set aside. Reduce the broth by at least half, then add the eggs into the boiling broth and stir until cooked.

Preheat oven to 425F. Butter a deep 12 inch round pan. Butter 5 phyllo sheets and arrange them around the edge of the pan. The sheets should be half in, half out, of the pan. Place one phyllo sheet in the middle of the pan. Place the chicken in the middle of the pan, spread out evenly over the base of the pan. Cover with the egg mixture. Sprinkle the almond mixture over the top. Place a buttered phyllo sheet over the top. Fold the outer edges of the base phyllo sheets over the middle, like the petals of a flower, to fully enclose the filling. Butter 5 more phyllo sheets. Carefully lift up the edge of the B'stila, lay half of one of the phyllo underneath, and fold the other half over the top for another set of petals. Continue with the rest of the phyllo.

Bake on the bottom rack of the oven for 15 minutes, then move to the middle rack for another 5 minutes. Remove from oven. Carefully slide the B'stila to a serving plate. Traditionally, icing sugar is sifted over the top and cinnamon lines are crisscrossed over that. I have omitted that step, and so did Lucy.

Baked Chicken with Cider and Apples

found this years ago in the Toronto Star, which had taken it from the *Silver Palate Good Times Cookbook*. It is a good dish for company; it tastes good, the flavours are unexpected, and it goes together quickly after marinating.

Two chickens, quartered or 12 chicken thighs

2 cups apple cider

1 cup all purpose flour

1 tbs brown ginger

2 tsp cinnamon

Salt and freshly ground black pepper

3 tbs brown sugar

1/3 cup Calvados or applejack

Two apples, cored and cut into thin wedges

One day before serving, place chicken pieces in a shallow dish. Poor cider over chicken and marinate overnight in the refrigerator, turning the pieces occasionally.

The next day, preheat oven to 350F. Remove chicken from dish and reserve cider. Mix flour, ginger, cinnamon and salt and pepper to taste. Dredge chicken in flour mixture and place skin side up in a baking pan. Bake uncovered for 40 minutes. Meanwhile, combine the reserved cider, brown sugar, Calvados and apple slices. At the 40 minute mark, pour over chicken and bake 25 minutes more, basting occasionally. Serve over a bed of egg noodles, or rice. You may thicken sauce with light table cream if you like.

Balsamic Chicken and Peppers

This is a very attractive dish to put out on a buffet or dinner table. The peppers and balsamic vinegar are a natural match. I found this on the Williams-Sonoma website. I have seasoned this with 1/2 tsp each dried basil and thyme when fresh herbs were not on hand.

4 boneless, skinless chicken breasts or about 8 thighs, about 1 1/2 lb in total

salt and freshly ground pepper to taste

4 tbsp olive oil

1 each red and yellow bell pepper, seeded and sliced

1 large yellow onion, thinly sliced

3 garlic cloves, minced

3 tbsp balsamic vinegar

1/4 cup minced fresh basil

1 tbsp minced fresh thyme

Season the chicken generously with salt and pepper. In a large fry pan over medium high heat, warm 2 tbs. of the olive oil. Add the chicken and cook, turning once, until golden brown, about 7 minutes total. Transfer to a plate. In the same pan over medium high heat, warm the remaining 2 tbs. olive oil. Add the bell peppers and onion, and sauté until softened, about 6 minutes. Add the garlic and sauté for 1 minute. Add the vinegar, half of the basil and half of the thyme and stir, scraping up the browned bits from the pan bottom. Return the chicken and any juices from the plate to the pan, spooning the peppers over the chicken. Reduce the heat to medium, and cook until the chicken is opaque throughout, 2 to 3 minutes. Stir in the remaining basil and thyme, and season with salt and pepper. Divide among 4 plates and serve immediately, or arrange on a serving dish for the table or buffet. Serves 4.

Chicken in Almond Sauce

I first made this in a very tiny kitchen in my apartment over the Mazurka Restaurant on rue Prince Arthur in Montreal. It took some serious organization and planning, as my single work surface was literally no more than two feet by two feet. I did not understand the limits of such a small space, but I made the dish anyway, and it turned out quite well. I took the recipe from Barbara Norman's *The Spanish Cookbook* (1971).

1 large chicken cut into small serving pieces

1 medium onion, chopped

2 cloves garlic, whole

12 peeled, toasted almonds

1 tablespoon flour for sauce, plus flour for dusting chicken

1 cup dry white wine

2 tablespoons dark rum

A small pinch of saffron, toasted and crushed

4 tablespoons olive oil

Salt and pepper to taste

Place saffron on a piece of parchment paper and toast lightly on a warm cast iron pan. Set aside. Cut chicken into small serving pieces. Dry thoroughly. Dip into flour, and sprinkle with salt and pepper. Fry slowly in hot olive oil with onion and whole garlic cloves. Meanwhile, boil water. When chicken is nicely browned, remove from pan along with the garlic. Stir saffron and 1 tablespoon flour into pan. Cook for one minute, then add white wine and rum. When the wine has reduced to half on a fairly fast boil, replace chicken. Pour in enough boiling water to cover. Season, add salt and pepper if necessary, and simmer, covered until meat is tender, up to one or two hours. Crush garlic cloves in mortar with almonds. Dilute with a little of the chicken sauce and stir it into the sauce in the casserole. Cook five minutes longer and serve. If sauce seems too thin, remove lid for the remainder of the cooking time.

Japanese Chicken Wings

I first tasted this at John and Nana's place in London. I asked Nana for the recipe and she showed me her copy of the *Prince George Peace River New Democrats Cookbook,* 1989. I bought the cookbook just to get this recipe. Then I read the recipe and thought the ingredient list was a misprint. It seemed impossible with the amount of sugar and butter it called for. I include the recipe for its sheer craziness. The final result is sticky and popular.

3 pounds chicken wings

1 cup flour

1 egg, beaten

1 cup butter

Sauce:

3 tbsp soy sauce

1/2 cup white vinegar

3 tbsp water

1/2 tsp salt

1 cup white sugar

Preheat oven to 350F. Cut the wings in half. Dip in egg and then flour. Fry in butter until deep brown and crisp. Put in a roasting pan. Mix ingredients for the sauce (soy sauce, water, sugar, vinegar, salt) and pour over the wings. Bake for one hour. Periodically spoon sauce over wings during cooking.

Oven Barbecued Chicken Wings

The first time I made oven barbecued chicken, I did not understand the possible effects of the combination of sweet sauce and hot chicken fat. I opened the oven door, pulled out the rack and leaned over to check it. The spitting fat set my hair on fire. Our friend watched this unfold and stepped forward to pour his beer over the chicken. "We'll have Belgian flamande instead" he said.

This recipe is safer, messy and good, and popular with guests. The ingredient list is simple, but this is the one method I have found that does not result in something burning.

2 lb chicken wings	1/2 cup barbecue sauce
salt and pepper	

Preheat oven to 375F. Lay wings out on parchment paper on a baking sheet. Roast for 45 minutes, turning once. Remove from oven and brush barbecue sauce over once side. Return to oven for 10 minutes. Remove from oven, turn over, and brush the other side with sauce. Return to oven and roast 10 minutes more. Remove from oven and serve.

Chapter 7

Fish

I have struggled with fish recipes, as the time line between over, under and just right baked or roasted fish can be a matter of only seconds. I have learned to look for small white lines emerging on salmon, and the right amount of flaking on the tines of a fork, but it is all about experience. My work arounds have included cooking fish in a stew or chowder, and soaking it in whiskey.

Irish Roasted Salmon

It may seem an indulgence to pour good whiskey over fish, but you could rationalize it by saying you really care about your dinner companions. I took this recipe from L*CBO's Food and Drink* Autumn 2003. I shared it with Brian Ridgley, who made it for his daughters at Christmas one year. In return, he gave me his recipe for Texas Chili (see Chapter 8)

2 tbsp honey

1/4 cup cider vinegar

1/4 cup Irish whiskey

2 tsp chopped fresh thyme

1 1/2 tsp grated lemon zest

2 tsp vegetable oil

salt & freshly ground pepper

4 salmon fillets, 6 oz. each

Mix together all ingredients except salmon fillets. Pour mixture over salmon and marinate one hour on the counter, or four hours in the refrigerator. Preheat oven to 450F. Remove salmon from marinade and place on rack in roasting pan. Bake for 10 to 12 minutes, basting once with marinade or until the salmon is golden and white juices are just beginning to appear.

Mediterranean Fish Chowder

Without the cheddar cheese, this is a classic, simple Mediterranean dish. As is the way with recipe evolution, someone thought some cheese would be good too.

1 medium or 2 small yellow onions, diced

6 ribs celery, chopped

6 cloves garlic, chopped

2 tablespoons olive oil

1 large tin diced tomatoes

2 tablespoons tomato paste

1 lb haddock, cod or other firm white fish, cut into 1 inch pieces

1/2 cup chicken broth

salt and pepper to taste

3/4 cup sharp cheddar cheese, grated

Sauté onion, celery and garlic in olive oil in large pot until onions are translucent. Stir in diced tomatoes and tomato paste, then add fish and broth. From this point onward, stir gently so as not to break up fish. When fish is cooked, stir in salt, pepper and cheese and heat through. Serve with crusty rolls or fresh sourdough bread.

Shrimp, Avocado and Tomato Salad

I wanted to make a light dinner salad for a friend. I found this recipe online, but I did not save the link and so I can not provide attribution. This is a recreated version. I spread the greens and shrimp out on a wide serving dish, and we ate it sitting at the picnic table under the trees in the backyard with a crisp white wine. Absolutely wonderful.

Vinaigrette for shrimp:

- 2 tbsp lime juice
- 2 tsp ground cumin
- 1 1/2 tsp grated lime zest
- 1 tsp minced garlic
- 1/2 tsp Dijon mustard
- 1/2 tsp salt
- 1/4 tsp ground black pepper
- 5 tbsp olive oil
- 24 large shrimp in the shell, about 1 1/4 lb

Salad:

- 2 ripe avocados
- 6 small tomatoes, any colour
- 3 tbsp chopped fresh cilantro
- 6 cups mixed salad greens

For the vinaigrette, whisk together lime juice, cumin, lime zest, garlic, mustard, salt and pepper, then slowly whisk in oil. Set aside. Bring a pot of water to boil, and cook the shrimp in the water until pink and curled, about 3 minutes. Drain, pat dry, shell and de-vein shrimp. Place the shrimp in a nonreactive bowl and pour half of the vinaigrette over. Let sit 10 minutes.

Halve, pit and slice avocados lengthwise, about 1/2 inch slices. Core and cut tomatoes into 1/2 inch wedges or slices. Add avocados, tomatoes and cilantro to shrimp and toss. Add the rest of the vinaigrette and toss. Spread the greens out over a wide serving dish. Pour shrimp, avocado, and tomato mixture over the greens and serve.

Baked Fish with Stuffing

You will find that some Mediterranean fish dishes have added fats, like cheese (this recipe) or meats (like paella). I thought it was just for flavour, but two vignettes tell a different story. Somewhere, I heard an old Greek man talk about adding olive oil to Greek salad "for the richness" and how important that was during the war (WWII). I thought that made sense; olive oil adds calories, and a nation in wartime typically suffers from food shortages. Olive oil would help bump the calorie content of a food into a healthier range.

The second time was when a kind Portuguese nurse was trying to explain to me how I should add more fish into my diet. She said the Portuguese do not eat only fish because, as their saying goes, "fish don't pull carts". She explained that eating only fish would not provide enough strength for heavy labour.

I remember making this at home when I was in my early teens, but the original recipe is long gone. The internet has a number of recipes for stuffed fish, chiefly from the Canadian Maritimes, that rely on crackers for the topping. The primary industry in the Maritimes is fishing, which is heavy work. This version is crunchy and has plenty of cheese.

2 8-ounce pieces of firm white fish, such as cod or haddock

salt and pepper

1 small yellow onion

1 tbsp unsalted butter

1 tbsp olive oil

1 tbsp Keen's dry mustard

2 cups fresh bread cubes

1 cup shredded white cheddar

Preheat oven to 400 F. Oil a baking pan, or line with parchment paper. Salt and pepper the fish fillets to taste. In a large fry pan, sauté the onion in the butter and oil until soft. Stir in dry mustard. Mix in bread crumbs, then cheddar. Pile the stuffing on top of the fish and bake for 20 minutes, or until fish flakes easily.

Chapter 8

Beef, Buffalo and Pork

Increasingly I substitute buffalo for beef; it's a leaner, sweeter meat. I also use pork, especially ground pork, more often as it is a much leaner product than what I grew up on in the 50's and 60's. A mixture of ground buffalo and pork is very good for meatballs and tourtiere. You can easily substitute ground beef in place of ground buffalo in any of these recipes.

Lorraine's Tourtiere

had tourtiere many times when growing up in Quebec; it is a traditional Christmas Eve dinner. I started looking for recipes both online and in books that combined the rustic nature of the dish, the thickening with potato, and the unexpected spice blend. I ended up developing this version because I keep ground buffalo in the freezer along with puff pastry. Pork nicely balances out the leanness of the bison.

1 lb. ground bison (or beef)	1/8-1/4 tsp freshly ground pepper
1 lb ground pork	2 bay leaves
1 tbsp oil	1 tsp salt
1 cup chopped onion	1 1/2 cups beef broth
2 large garlic cloves, chopped	1 medium and 1 small potato, peeled and grated
1/4 tsp each allspice & cinnamon	1 pkg puff pastry, thawed
1/8 tsp freshly ground nutmeg	1 egg beaten with 1 tbsp water

Brown the bison or beef and pork in a frying pan with the oil. When the meat is no longer pink, add onion and garlic. Cook 5 – 10 minutes until onion softens. Add spices and stir. Add broth and bay leaves. Bring to a simmer. Stir in potatoes and cook about 15 minutes until liquid is absorbed but the mixture is not dry. Remove bay leaves. Cool thoroughly and chill in the refrigerator for about 2 hours.

Preheat oven to 375F. Roll chilled meat into a log shape, about 12" long, on wax paper. Roll out half of puff pastry into a base rectangle about 16" by 8". You will want the base pastry to be 2" longer than the meat on each side. Place base pastry on a sheet of parchment paper, and move that on to a baking sheet. Place meat log on base pastry. Brush some of the egg wash on the rim of the base layer of pastry, to act as a sealant. Roll the rest of the puff pastry out to a rectangle, a little longer and wider than the base sheet, and place over base and meat. Press edges to seal, then trim to leave a generous 1 1/2 to 2" edge. Make small slashes on top pastry to release steam. Brush egg wash over entire surface of pastry.

Bake until puffed and golden brown, about 45 minutes. Slice and serve with chili sauce.

Texas Chili

This recipe was from Brian Ridgley, a big-hearted man who hired me for my first real job as a Neuropsychologist when he was head of the Psychology Department at a Toronto hospital. He spent a lot of time in Texas in the years I knew him, and went so far as to call his dog Austin. This is how he made his chili.

2 lb stewing beef

1 cup flour seasoned with salt and pepper

1 chopped Spanish onion

3 cloves garlic

2 cups beef broth

1 large tin crushed tomatoes

2 tbsp balsamic vinegar

1 - 2 tbsp cumin

2 tsp crushed red chili peppers, more or less

1 small tin green peppers, chopped

salt and pepper as desired

Dredge beef in flour seasoned with salt and pepper. In a large pot, fry onions in oil until lightly browned, then sauté garlic briefly without browning. Season with salt and pepper. Remove onions and garlic from pot. Add beef and brown, in batches. Remove from pot. Pour beef broth into pot and bring to a boil. Deglaze the pan by bringing the liquid to a boil and scraping up the browned bits as they soften. Add the beef and onions back to the pot. Add tomatoes, vinegar, cumin, chili peppers and green peppers. Simmer several hours. Serve garnished with sliced avocados and sour cream, and cornbread on the side.

Buffet Meatballs

Last December, we held a Christmas season open house. I made these meatballs because I had jars of Green Tomato Jam (see chapter 11) and thought it would make a good base for a meatball sauce for a buffet dish. I adapted this meatball recipe from the Canadian Living website.

Meatballs:

1 egg	1 tsp grated ginger root
1/4 cup dry breadcrumbs	1/2 tsp salt
1/4 cup finely chopped green onion	1/4 tsp pepper
2 tbsp grated carrot	1 lb lean ground pork

Preheat oven to 375F. Beat egg until frothy then add all ingredients. Blend all ingredients together and form into small meatballs, a generous tablespoon each. Bake on rimmed, parchment lined tray for about 15 minutes, or until no longer pink inside. The recipe for Meatball Sauce is also in Chapter 11.

Sauce:

1 1/2 cups Green Tomato Jam (see Chapter 11 Miscellany)	Than Bouillon brand concentrate)
1 1/2 cups beef broth (I use Better	2 tbsp corn starch
	2 tbsp water

Warm the tomato jam and bouillon in a pan. Stir together the cornstarch and water in a small bowl. Stir that into the warmed jam and bouillon mix, and bring to a boil. Cook for about one minute, until thickened and glossy.

Place meatballs in casserole, pour sauce over, serve with toothpicks on the side.

Soba Noodles with Pork

It is easy to change this recipe to suit what you have on hand. I had some boneless pork chops, which I marinated, fried and cut in strips. The hot pork over cold spicy noodles made for a very pleasant meal on the front porch on a summer day. This suited the tastes of house guests and neighborhood friends.

Marinade for pork:

3 tbsp green onions, chopped

2 tbsp sesame oil, divided

4 tsp fish sauce, divided

1 tbsp soy sauce

2 tsp brown sugar

1/2 tsp ground pepper

1 lb boneless pork loin, trimmed and cut into 1/2 inch thick strips OR 4 to 6 boneless pork chops, left whole

Noodles:

8 ounces soba noodles, cooked and drained

2 tbsp rice wine vinegar

1 tsp chili paste with garlic

3 cups chopped Napa cabbage

1/2 cup finely chopped red bell pepper

Combine 1 tbsp onion, 1 tbsp sesame oil, 1 tsp fish sauce and soy sauce, brown sugar, pepper and pork in a large zip top baggie; seal. Marinate in refrigerator for at least 20 minutes, or up to several hours.

Cook noodles according to package directions. Drain. Combine remaining 1 tbsp oil, remaining 1 tbsp fish sauce, vinegar and chili paste in a large bowl, stirring well. Add noodles, cabbage and bell pepper; toss to coat. Heat a skillet over medium high heat. Coat pan with cooking spray or a small dollop of oil. Remove pork from marinade. Add pork to pan; cook 1 1/2 minutes, turning once, or until done. If using pork chops, cook longer until no longer pink inside. Slice cooked chops into strips.

Place noodles on serving platter. Arrange pork over noodle mixture and serve.

Chapter 9

Pies and Pastry

struggled for a long time to get pastry right. I usually under floured when rolling out, which meant pastry dough sticking to everything in sight and becoming a ragged mess on the pie, or undercooking which resulted in a pale, cardboard like pastry. I liked graham wafer crusts and streusel pie topping as a way to avoid pastry. I always worried about the admonition in books: "do not use too much flour, or the pastry will be tough". They did not warn about using too little. If ever you have rolled out some store bought puff pastry dough, you will understand exactly the right texture for pastry. It is necessary to put enough flour on the work surface, and the rolling pin, so that rolling is clean and does not stick. When you get to that point, just stop flouring the surface and the pin. The second problem I ran into was under baking. My pies were pale and tasteless. I read recipes that spoke of brushing milk on top for browning, and sprinkling sugar for taste, so I just assumed everyone else had the same problem as me. I finally learned to add a little more flour, and bake longer, and my pies were better.

Buttery Pie Pastry

This pastry recipe and the Peach Pie recipe later in the chapter were adapted from Smitten Kitchen and Good Life Farm. Makes a double 9 inch pie crust.

2 1/2 cups whole wheat flour

1 tablespoon sugar

1 teaspoon salt

2 sticks (8 ounces, 16 tablespoons or 1 cup) unsalted butter, very cold

1/2 – 1 cup ice cold water

Cut two sticks of very cold unsalted butter into 1/2 inch pieces and put them in the freezer for a few minutes. Pour a cup of cold water into a bowl and drop in a few ice cubes; set aside. In a large bowl, whisk together whole wheat flour, 1 tablespoon of sugar and a teaspoon of salt. Take the butter pieces out of the freezer, sprinkle over the flour, and begin working them in with a pastry blender or two knives until the butter pieces are the size of tiny peas. Drizzle 1/2 cup of the ice cold water over the butter and flour mixture.

Using a spatula, gather the dough together. You may need up to an additional 1/4 cup of cold water to bring it together, but add it a tablespoon as a time. As the dough starts to come together, take it out of the bowl and begin kneading it gently and quickly together. The dough is wet and sticky at this stage, but it works in the end. So go ahead, add that much water, even if it seems like too much at the time.

Divide the dough in half, and wrap each half in plastic wrap. Let the dough chill in the refrigerator for one hour, preferably at least two, before rolling it out. Dough will keep in the refrigerator for about a week, and longer in the freezer. If not using it that day, wrap it in additional layers of plastic wrap. To defrost your dough, move it to the refrigerator for one day before using it.

Aunt Thelma's Never Fail Pie Pastry

This is a terrific recipe for a starter cook just learning how to manage pastry dough. Roll and re-roll as you might, it will never get tough. Makes 2 9 inch pie shells.

2 cups sifted flour

1 cup shortening

1 tsp salt

1 tbsp vinegar

1/3 cup cold milk

To sour the milk with the vinegar, pour the vinegar in a bowl or measuring cup, pour the milk on top, and leave it about 10 minutes. Sift the flour and salt together and cut in shortening until fine. Add milk and stir until well combined. Flour a work surface and a rolling pin, and roll out as needed.

Ham, Cheese and Vegetable Pub Pie

This is another pie I made while in Ottawa during the early 1990's. It was clipped from a magazine which I cannot remember. I made it for a brunch for extended family. The wedges of pie with the red pepper are quite pretty on the plate.

Pastry:

2 cup all purpose flour

1/2 tsp salt

1/3 cup lard

3 tbsp butter

3 to 4 tbsp water

Combine flour and salt in mixing bowl. Rub in lard and butter with fingers until the mixture resembles fine crumbs. Work in enough water to form soft dough. This recipe works well in a food processor. Wrap the dough and chill while you chop the vegetables.

Cut off 1/3 of chilled dough and set aside. Roll out the rest to fit an 8-inch spring form pan, with the dough overhanging the edges.

Filling:

2 tbsp oil or butter

1 onion, finely chopped

2 sticks celery, chopped

1/2 cup chopped mushrooms

2 300 gram (about 1 1/2 lb total) packages frozen chopped spinach, thawed

100 grams (about 1/4 lb) sliced ham

1 1/2 cups shredded mozzarella or Swiss cheese

1 500 ml (about 1 cup) jar sweet red peppers

1/2 tsp salt

1/2 tsp pepper

a pinch each of sage and thyme (about 1/8 tsp)

6 eggs

Preheat oven to 400F. Sauté onion and celery in oil or butter for 2 to 3 minutes. Add mushrooms and cook another 2 to 3 minutes. Squeeze as much moisture as possible from thawed spinach. Add spinach to pan, and stir to combine. Remove from heat. Cut the ham in 1 inch strips. Lay half of the ham in bottom of pastry-lined pan. Top with half the cheese, then half of the spinach mixture. Sprinkle half of the salt, pepper, spices and then layer on all of the red peppers. Repeat the layers. Beat the eggs well and pour over the filling.

Roll out the rest of the pastry into an 8 inch round or larger. Lay on top of the pie and pinch the edges firmly to seal. Cut out shapes from the scraps to decorate the top of the pie, and affix them with some beaten egg. Brush the surface with a little beaten egg or milk. Bake for 50 minutes. You may slip the ring of the springform pan off for the last 10 minutes to brown the sides. Cool for at least 10 minutes before serving.

Peach Pie

As time goes by, I cook with less sugar. One August I went looking for a low-sugar peach pie recipe, and made this. Fresh Niagara peaches in August do not need a lot of extra sweetener.

Pastry for a double 9" pie crust

Filling:

About 3 1/2 pounds peaches (approximately 7 medium)

1 tbsp lemon juice, about half a regular lemon

1/4 cup brown sugar

1/4 tsp cinnamon

1/8 tsp nutmeg

1/8 tsp table salt

3 tablespoons cornstarch

Finish:

1 tbsp milk

1 tbsp coarse or granulated sugar

Bring a large saucepan of water to boil. Prepare an ice bath. Make a small x at the bottom of each peach. Once water is boiling, lower as many peaches as you can fit at once into saucepan and poach for two to three minutes. Using a slotted spoon, transfer to ice bath for one minute to cool. Transfer peaches to cutting board and peel off the skins. You may need to use a paring knife.

Halve and pit the peaches, then cut into slices about 1/3 inch thick to make 6 to 7 cups. Put in a large bowl and toss with lemon juice. In a small dish, stir together sugar, cinnamon, nutmeg, salt and corn starch until evenly mixed. Add to peaches and toss to coat evenly.

Preheat the oven to 425 F. Roll out one ball of pastry dough on a generously floured surface and place in 9" pie pan. Fill the bottom crust with your reserved peach filling. Roll out the rest of the dough to make the top crust. Lay the second layer of pie crust on top, and make holes to let steam escape. Trim and seal the edge. To finish, brush pie with milk and sprinkle with sugar (optional).

Bake for about 20 minutes until the crust is set and beginning to brown. Reduce oven temperature to 375 and bake pie for another 30 to 40 minutes until filling is bubbling and the crust is golden brown. Cool for three hours at room temperature before serving.

Pumpkin Pie

I clipped this recipe from the Toronto Star. I can't remember when I found it, but I remember making it in Ottawa when I was in grad school in the early 90's. The pastry, especially the bottom, is very flaky and the filling is wonderful. I served it with whipped cream which had a wee splash of Poire William, a pear liqueur, and the entire thing was wonderful. You can omit the liqueur if children are going to be eating this.

pastry for a 9 inch pie

beaten egg

Filling:

1 cup dark brown sugar

a pinch of salt (about 1/8 tsp)

1 tbsp all purpose flour

2 tsp cinnamon

1 tsp ground ginger

1/2 tsp each cloves, allspice and freshly ground nutmeg

3 eggs, beaten

1 14 oz can mashed pumpkin (2 cups)

1 1/2 cups milk

2 to 3 tbsp brandy or rum, optional

whipped cream for garnish

Line a deep 9 inch pie plate with pastry. Flute edges (that means crimp the sides so they stand up a little) and brush bottom of pastry with beaten egg. Refrigerate.

For the filling, combine sugar, salt, flour and spices. Blend and make a well in the middle. Stir in beaten eggs. Combine pumpkin and milk, then add to the spice mixture. Add brandy or rum, if using. Chill well.

When you are ready to bake, preheat oven to 450F.

Pour the chilled pumpkin mixture into the pie shell. Bake for 10 minutes, then lower heat to 400F and bake for 10 minutes. Lower heat again to 350F and bake 30 to 35 minutes, or until set. Let cool to room temperature. Serve with whipped cream.

Graham Wafer Pie (Flapper Pie)

This pie was the first time my brother and I had tasted a graham wafer crust. The pie became known in our house as Graham Wafer Pie. It was my brother's favourite when we were kids. I believe this custard recipe was on the back of the Graham Wafer Cracker box. I wrote the recipe out on a Honey Bee Graham Wafer index card, and from the handwriting, I was about 12 years old. This is also known as Flapper Pie on the Prairies.

Crust:

2 cups graham wafer crumbs

1 tsp cinnamon

1/2 cup melted butter

Filling:

2 cups milk

pinch salt

3 egg yolks

1 tbsp butter

5 tbsp white sugar

1 tsp vanilla

2 1/2 tbsp cornstarch

Meringue:

3 egg whites

2 tbsp white sugar

Preheat oven to 325F. To make the crust, mix graham wafer crumbs, butter and cinnamon together. Set aside 2 tablespoons to sprinkle over meringue. Press the rest of the mixture firmly into the bottom and sides of a 9 inch pie pan. Bake at 325F for 10 minutes, then cool and chill before filling.

Turn oven down to 300F.

To make the filling, mix milk, sugar, salt and cornstarch in a heavy sauce pan. Cook, stirring constantly, until it begins to thicken. Remove from heat. Beat egg yolks lightly. Add a few spoonfuls of hot milk mixture to egg yolks, stir in well, then slowly add yolks back into hot milk mixture, stirring constantly. Return to heat and cook, stirring constantly, until mixture bubbles. Remove from heat and immediately add in butter and vanilla. Stir to combine. Pour into baked crust.

To make the meringue, beat egg whites until soft peaks form, then beat in sugar until stiff peaks form. Spread over pie. Sprinkle reserved crumbs over top. and put into 300F oven 12 to 15 minutes to brown the meringue. Let cool, then chill before serving.

Lemon Meringue Pie

A lot of my basic pie knowledge came from Mom's copy of the *Purity Flour Cookbook* circa 1947. It was given to her when she married. She did not know how to make pie, and relied on this book to teach her. She said the first year of marriage in 1947 saw some bad pies, but she persevered and it ended up well.

1 baked pie shell (Roll out pastry dough for a 9 inch pie plate and prick all over with a fork to let steam escape. Put in 425F oven and bake 12 to 15 minutes until lightly browned.)

Filling:

1 cup sugar	2 cups boiling water
6 tbsp flour	1 tbsp butter
1/2 tsp salt	2 egg whites
2 egg yolks	2 to 3 tbsp sugar
juice and grated rind of 1 lemon	

Preheat oven to 300F. In a heavy saucepan, mix sugar, flour and salt together. Beat egg yolks until creamy, then stir in lemon juice and rind. Stir lemon mixture into flour mixture and mix until smooth. Gradually add boiling water and cook in a double boiler for 10 minutes, or until thickened. Add butter, stir until melted and pour into pie shell.

Beat two egg whites until soft peaks form, then beat in sugar until stiff peaks form. Cover the pie. Bake for 12 to 15 minutes until meringue is delicately browned. Cool to room temperature before serving.

Chocolate Cream Pie

This is also from the *Purity Flour Cookbook* ca 1947. The chocolate filling is rich and fudge-like in flavour.

1 baked pie shell (Roll out pastry dough for a 9 inch pie plate and prick all over with a fork to let steam escape. Put in 425F oven and bake 12 to 15 minutes until lightly browned.)

Filling:

2 ounces unsweetened chocolate	1/4 cup cold milk
1 cup hot milk	2 egg yolks
4 tbsp flour	1/2 tsp vanilla
3/4 cup white sugar	2 egg whites
1/2 tsp salt	2 – 3 tbsp sugar

Heat milk in a heavy saucepan. Grate chocolate into hot milk and beat until smooth. In a separate bowl, mix flour, sugar, salt and cold milk then add to the hot milk mixture. Cook for about 15 minutes, stirring constantly until thickened. Beat the egg yolks, adding a couple spoons of the hot custard while stirring, then slowly pour the yolks back into the custard while stirring constantly. Cook another 2 to 3 minutes, stirring constantly. Remove from heat and stir in vanilla. Pour into the baked pie shell. Allow to cool slightly while making meringue.

Preheat oven to 300F. Beat two egg whites until soft peaks form, then beat in sugar until stiff peaks form. Pile meringue on to pie and bake for 12 to 15 minutes so that meringue is a delicate brown. Allow to cool to room temperature before serving.

Chapter 10

Desserts

I have collected a lot more dessert recipes than anything else. I think that because, while I can ad lib recipes for a casserole, party dip or salad, I need good, clear recipes for baking. I hang on to the ones I like, because I can not re-create them on my own, and baking recipes are not too forgiving of changes.

Section 1: Cookies

Basic Refrigerator Cookie

This is one of the first recipes I collected in the mid 1960's from an ad in a magazine. What was unusual for the time was that it specified butter, not margarine. You can do quite a lot with this recipe by mixing in different flavourings and additions. It is really handy to have a log of cookie dough in the freezer, ready to go for any occasion. Makes 5 dozen.

Cookie Dough:

2/3 cup butter	2 cups all purpose flour
1 cup brown sugar	1/4 tsp salt
1 egg	1/2 tsp baking soda
1 tsp vanilla	

Cream the butter and gradually add in brown sugar. Then beat in egg and vanilla. Mix together flour, salt and baking soda and mix into butter mixture.

You can proceed at this point to a basic sugar cookie or add in one of the following 5 variations, or make up your own:

1 ounce (square) melted semisweet baking chocolate and 4 tbsp chopped nuts

or

1/2 cup chopped mixed peel

or

1/2 tsp almond extract, and roll log in finely chopped almonds

or

1/2 tsp coconut flavouring, and roll log in sweetened desiccated coconut

or

1/4 cup each dried cranberries and chopped pistachios

Whichever way you flavour it, roll the dough into a log. Wrap the dough in plastic wrap and shape into a uniform cylinder using a straight edge such as the side of a knife, pan, or ruler. Flatten the ends and place in the freezer to store, or refrigerator to chill.

To bake, preheat the oven to 350F. Slice the dough thinly and lay on a greased cookie sheet, or lined with parchment paper or silicone sheet. Bake for 8 – 10 minutes.

Orange Marmalade Cookies

I found quite a few versions of Marmalade cookies on the internet, and liked this one the best. There is no added sugar in this recipe. The idea has been around for a long time. The story told is that Marmalade cookies were developed in post-war Britain when sugar was scarce. The cookie has a pleasant, mild orange flavour and is not overly sweet. I have substituted whole wheat flour for white flour on occasion. Makes 2 dozen.

1/2 cup butter	1 tsp vanilla
1 egg	2 cups all purpose flour
1 cup orange marmalade – but any type of marmalade will work	1 tsp salt
	1 tsp baking soda

Preheat the over to 350F. Cream the butter, marmalade and egg together. Mix in vanilla. Sift together flour, salt and baking powder and stir into butter mixture. Drop by spoonfuls onto greased or lined cookie sheets, 2" apart. Bake for 12 – 15 minutes or until lightly browned.

Pine Nut Cookies

I wanted to make an authentic Italian cookie for my sister in law at Christmas, and found this recipe online. It is adapted from Giada Di Laurentiis on the Food Network. It is another less sweet cookie.

1/2 cup butter at room temperature	1 large egg
1/2 cup plus 2 tbsp sugar	1 1/4 cups all purpose flour
1 tsp vanilla	1/4 cup pine nuts
1/4 tsp salt	

Beat together the butter and sugar, then add in egg and vanilla and beat again. Add in flour and salt and mix just until blended. Place the dough on a sheet of plastic wrap and form into a log. Wrap and place in refrigerator to chill for two hours.

To bake, preheat oven to 350F. Line baking sheets with parchment paper. Slice dough into 1/4 to 1/8 inch slices. Press a pine nut into the top of each cookie. Bake about 15 minutes, until golden along the edges.

Lemon Ricotta Cookies

The same year I was looking for authentic Italian cookies for my sister in law's Christmas party (see Pine Nut Cookies), I found this recipe. My sister in law, and her Italian mother, loved these and now ask for them at Christmas.

1/2 cup butter	3 tbsp lemon juice
2 cups sugar	finely grated zest of one lemon
2 eggs	2 1/2 cups flour
1 15 ounce container whole milk ricotta cheese	1 tsp baking powder
	1 tsp salt

Beat the butter and sugar together very well, about 3 minutes. Add in eggs, one at a time and beat after each addition. Add in ricotta, lemon juice and lemon zest. Sift together flour, baking powder and salt, and stir into the butter mixture.

Preheat oven to 375F and grease or line baking sheets with parchment paper. Drop about 2 tbsp of dough per cookie onto sheet. Bake for about 15 minutes, until slightly golden at the edges. Let the cookies cool another 20 minutes on the baking sheets before removing them.

Some recipes suggest a glaze on the cookies. I glazed these the first time I made them, and found them too sweet for my taste. I have not glazed them since, which allows the subtle flavours to come forward.

Oat Flour Chocolate Chip Cookies

I went through a gluten-free phase a few years back but I really missed chocolate chip cookies. I adapted this from Martha Stewart's recipe for gluten-free chocolate chip cookies. This has become my favourite chocolate chip recipe, because it is a less sweet version than the Tollhouse version I used for years. Note the use of dark chocolate chips- it makes a big difference. Makes about 4 dozen cookies.

4 1/2 cups long cooking oats

1 1/2 tsp cinnamon

1/2 tsp salt

1 tsp baking powder

2 tbsp cornstarch

1 cup unsalted butter (2 sticks) at room temperature

1/2 cup packed light brown sugar

3/4 cup granulated sugar

2 eggs

2 tsp vanilla

3/4 cup dark chocolate chips (50% or more cacao)

Preheat the oven to 350F. Put 1 1/2 cups of the long cooking oats in a blender or food processor and process into a fine oat flour. Whisk the oat flour, cornstarch, cinnamon, baking powder and salt together. In the bowl of a stand mixer, beat together butter and sugars until light and fluffy. Beat in eggs and vanilla. With mixers on low, gradually add in oat flour mixture until combined. Fold in chocolate chips and remaining 3 cups of oats.

Line baking sheets with parchment paper. Drop 2 tbsp of dough onto sheet, 2 inches apart. Bake 15 – 18 minutes, until edges are golden brown. Let cool on sheet on a wire rack for 2 minutes, then transfer to rack to cool completely.

Jam Buttons

This is another blast from the past. They are also known as Birds' Nests and Thumb Print Cookies. The cookie is buttery, the jam is sweet and the nuts are crunchy. The combination is terrific. Makes four dozen.

1 cup unsalted butter

1 cup sugar

1/2 tsp salt

2 tsp vanilla extract

2 egg yolks

2 2/3 cups flour

Raspberry preserves (or any jam or jelly)

Two egg whites, beaten

about 2 cups chopped walnuts or almonds.

Preheat oven to 350°F. Cream the butter and sugar together until light and fluffy. Beat in the salt, vanilla and egg yolks. Mix in flour. Roll the dough, about 1 tablespoon at a time, into balls. Roll in beaten egg white and then in nuts. Put on ungreased baking sheet. Press down in the middle of each cookie with your thumb. Fill centre of each cookie with 1/4 teaspoon of jam. Bake for 15 minutes, until the edge of the cookie is lightly browned.

Oatmeal Jam-Jams

These were my brother's favourite cookie was he was a little boy. Our Grandmother Jordan shared the recipe with her daughters and daughters in law, but the story goes that nobody could reproduce this cookie. Their versions always came out flat and hard. Sometime after my grandmother's passing, I received her day-to-day working cookbook, and I found a recipe that had been marked off with wavy pen lines. It was called "Thin Oatmeal Cookies" from Margo Oliver's Weekend Magazine Cookbook (1967). The recipe called for the cookies to be sandwiched together with date filling, but Grandma always used jam.

So, I made this recipe and added between 1/4 and 1/2 cup milk to the dough, which produced a fluffy, soft cookie. That was the missing element in Grandma's recipe! I sandwiched them together with jam, and rolled them in icing sugar, like Grandma Jordan had. They tasted authentic to my brother and I. This recipe will make 12 dozen single cookies, or 6 dozen pairs.

1 cup soft shortening	1 tsp soda
1 cup packed brown sugar	1 tsp salt
3 cups rolled oats	1/2 cup water
2 cups sifted all purpose flour	1/4 to 1/2 cup milk

Preheat oven to 375F. Mix the shortening and sugar together and 1/4 cup of milk. If dough is too dry, add the extra 1/4 cup milk and mix well. Drop dough by spoonfuls onto greased cookie sheet and bake for about 10 minutes, until lightly browned. Glue two cookies together at the base with jam. Grandma Jordan rolled them in icing sugar, but you can omit that step if it seems too sweet.

Lorraine's Oatmeal Cookies

In the early 1970's I started writing recipes in a notebook, including this one, which I had written up with my name. I do not remember if I generated the recipe on my own, but oatmeal cookie recipes can be very similar, and I might have copied it. When I made the recipe again in 2019, I liked it a lot and decided to include it here. Makes 3 dozen.

1 cup butter	1/2 tsp salt
1/2 cup white sugar	1 tsp cinnamon
1 cup brown sugar	1 1/2 cups rolled oats
2 beaten eggs	1 1/2 tsp vanilla
1 1/2 cups flour	1/2 cup each chopped walnuts and chocolate chips
1 tsp baking soda	

Preheat oven to 350F. Cream together butter and sugars, then beaten eggs. Stir in flour, soda, salt, cinnamon and vanilla. Stir in rolled oats, nuts and chocolate chips. Drop by rounded spoonfuls onto greased pans. Bake for 10 to 15 minutes, until golden brown.

Austrian Vanilla Crescents / Vanillekipferl

This is another recipe I first made in the mid 1980s, but I do not recall the source. I had to have found it in a book or magazine because there was no internet. This is a very simple cookie: butter, sugar and nuts, with some flour to bind it all together. Makes 2 1/2 dozen.

1 cup cold butter

1 1/4 cup all-purpose flour

1/2 cup very finely ground almonds
    or hazelnuts

1/2 cup granulated sugar

Powdered sugar or powdered vanilla
    sugar

Preheat oven to 275F. Rub the butter into flour by hand. Gradually work in almonds and sugar. Shape a piece of dough the size of a walnut into a crescent shape. Bake on cookie sheet for about a half hour until set, but not brown. While warm, roll in powdered sugar. Traditionally, this cookie is rolled in powdered vanilla sugar, which can be found in specialty European-style food shops. If you can not find it, use plain powdered sugar

Tommy Douglas Cookies

I have a number of cookbooks that are fundraiser collections. Irma Douglas, wife of Tommy Douglas, submitted this recipe to a collection published by the Prince George Peace River New Democrats in 1989. Tommy Douglas is famous in Canada as the creator of Canada's universal health care system. She described these as her husband's favourite cookie, hence the name I use here. She said that Tommy always liked a little more coconut. She kept a jar of these on hand. Makes 6 dozen cookies.

1 cup white sugar

1 cup brown sugar

1 cup butter softened

2 large eggs

2 tsp baking soda

1 tsp salt

2 cups all purpose flour

1 1/2 tsp vanilla

1/4 cup flaked coconut or more, up to 1 cup

3 cups rolled oats

1 cup peanuts, dates or raisins. (Peanuts are preferred in our house)

Preheat oven to 350F. The original recipe says to mix the ingredients together in order, one at a time, leaving the rolled oats until last. I mix the sugars and butter together using a stand mixer, then beat in the eggs and vanilla until the batter is light and fluffy. Stir in the flour, salt and soda, mix well, then stir in coconut, oats and peanuts. Roll about 2 tablespoons of the dough into balls and place on lightly greased cookie sheet. Pat down slightly. Bake for 10 or 11 minutes.

Gerta's Linzer Cookies

Gerta was a medical student from Austria who spent a year in London, Ontario back in the 80's. Her partner was spending the year training in the Neurology research lab where I worked at the time. She brought these cookies and truffles to my wedding shower, and they disappeared fast. She very kindly shared the recipe with me. The recipe is reproduced as she gave it to me. When I make it, I use a kitchen scale to measure the weight of the nuts and butter.

140 g flour (or 7/8 cup)

140 g brown sugar (3/4 cup) brown sugar

1/2 teaspoon each of cinnamon and cloves

2 egg yolks

140 g of finely chopped almonds

140 g of butter (one stick plus a little more)

100 g semisweet chocolate very finely chopped

Put all the ingredients together and knead until the dough is firm. Chill for about one half hour.

Preheat oven to 300F. Roll the dough to about 1/8 inch thick and cut out round cookies. Make a smaller hole in one half the cookies. Bake for 10 or 11 minutes. Put a small amount of raspberry or apricot jam on a whole cookie, and top with a cookie with a hole in it.

Gerta's Chocolate Truffles

Gerta also brought these to the party. This is a pretty straightforward truffle recipe; the results are fantastic when using the best quality chocolate you can find.

8 ounces semi sweet chocolate

4 ounces sweet chocolate

1 can sweetened condensed milk

1 cup very finely chopped almonds

1 or 2 tablespoons of Grand Marnier or Cointreau

Note: if you use liqueur, reduce the amount of milk by the same amount

Melt chocolates together over very low heat, stirring constantly. Add milk and liqueur and mix until smooth. Cool slightly, shape into balls and roll in nuts.

Section 2: Squares and Bars

Walnut Date Bars

I developed these bars so that I could take a fast and healthy snack to work. I adapted the recipe from the internet. They are dense, chewy and crunchy all at once, and do not require any special handling beyond wrapping in a twist of wax paper. Some dried cranberries are sold prepackaged with additional sugar, which I find adds too much sweetness to the recipe. If you cannot find plain dried cranberries, substitute a different dried fruit, such as cherries, blueberries or raisins.

1 1/2 cups walnuts, chopped

1/3 cup whole wheat flour

1/8 tsp each baking powder and
   baking soda

1/4 tsp salt

1/2 tsp cinnamon

1/3 cup brown sugar

2 cups dates, pitted and chopped

1/2 cup dried cranberries

1 egg

1 tsp vanilla

Preheat oven to 325F. Mix the chopped dates and whole dried cranberries together and set aside. Line an 8 x 8" pan with parchment paper, with extra length to hang over sides. Place flour, salt, baking powder, baking soda and cinnamon in food processor and process briefly to blend. Add in half of the dried fruit and process to chop the fruit further and coat with flour. Pour the flour and fruit mixture into a larger bowl and stir in the rest of the fruit by hand. Beat together vanilla and egg and pour into centre of fruit and flour mixture. Stir to mix thoroughly. The mixture will be very loose. Pour into the square pan and pat down firmly by hand, or with the bottom of a glass. Bake for 30 minutes.

Brownies

This recipe is taken directly from the *Purity Cookbook* ca 1947. It is the one my brother and I grew up with, and was one of the first recipes I learned to make. In the early learning stages, I stirred the melting chocolate with a plastic spoon, which melted. I was left with a plastic stub in my hand. I was not sure if I should go ahead at that point, but I did give it some thought, and went and asked my father. Since he was a Chemical Engineer, I thought he would know. He did not think I should use the chocolate plastic mixture.

1/2 cup butter	1/2 cup walnuts or pecans
1 cup white sugar	1 cup flour
2 eggs	1/8 tsp salt
2 squares (1 ounce each) baking chocolate, melted	1/2 tsp vanilla

Preheat oven to 350F. Melt the chocolate and set aside to cool. Cream the butter and sugar. Beat in the eggs. Stir in the melted chocolate. Stir in the flour, salt, and walnuts. Bake in a greased 8" x 8" pan for 20 to 25 minutes.

Lower Fat Fudge Brownies

As I got older, I started to bargain with reality with recipes like this: a lower fat brownie. While I shake my head a little at the contradiction now, at the time it seemed like a good idea. Unexpectedly this turned out to be a really good brownie. The recipe comes from *Let Them Eat Cake* by Susan Purdy.

cooking spray (butter flavour recommended)

1/4 cup unsalted butter (1/2 stick) cut up

1 ounce unsweetened chocolate, chopped

1 cup minus 2 tbsp sifted cake flour

1/2 cup unsifted unsweetened Dutch-processed cocoa powder

1/4 tsp baking powder

1/4 tsp salt

1/8 tsp cinnamon

a generous pinch of freshly ground nutmeg

1 1/4 cups granulated sugar

1 large egg plus 2 egg whites

1 tbsp vanilla extract

3 tbsp water

Position a rack in the middle of the oven and preheat to 350F. Lightly coat an 8 x 8" baking pan with cooking spray. Combine the chopped chocolate and butter in a small pan and gently heat over low heat to melt the chocolate. Stir the mixture to blend and set aside to cool. In a medium sized bowl, whisk together the flour, cocoa, baking powder, salt, cinnamon and nutmeg. Put the sugar in the bowl of a stand mixture and pour in the butter-chocolate mixture. Add the egg, egg whites, vanilla and water and beat well. Add the dry ingredients and blend slowly just until mixed. Do not over mix. The batter will be thick. Spoon it into the baking pan and smooth the top. Bake for 22 to 25 minutes. When done, the top will look dry and a wooden toothpick stuck in near the side will come out with a few crumbs. The centre will look gooey. Cool in the pan before cutting into squares.

Caramel Pecan Shortbread Bars

I make this every year at Christmas, as it is the time of year when we indulge in richer foods. One has to get through the winter, after all. This recipe is from Susan Mendelson's *The Lazy Gourmet*, printed in The Toronto Star February 15, 1989. These bars always get rave reviews and requests for the recipe.

Shortbread base:

1 cup unsalted butter	1 tsp lemon juice
6 tbsp brown sugar	3 cups flour
1 egg	

Pecans:

3 cups pecans

Topping:

3/4 cup butter	3/4 cup brown sugar
7 tbsp honey	3 tbsp heavy cream

Preheat oven to 350F. Line a 10 x 15" pan with parchment paper, with extra paper hanging over to help removal later. Blend the shortbread ingredients in a food processor, with an electric beater, or by hand. Press into pan. Prick all over with a fork to allow steam to escape and prevent buckling. Bake for 20 minutes and remove from oven when lightly browned and spread the pecans over the base.

For the topping, in a heavy saucepan, melt butter with honey. Add sugar and bring to a boil, cooking until dark brown, 5 to 7 minutes, whisking continuously. Remove from heat and add cream immediately. Stir to combine and pour over pecans. Return shortbread to oven and bake 20 minutes longer. Allow to cool to room temperature before cutting into bars. The caramel will glue the pecans to the shortbread, creating a new version of an old Southern favourite.

Section 3: Cakes

Macaroon Cake or Cupcakes

A retro touch, these were popular in their day. This makes a beautiful, old fashioned cake or cupcake. The flavour and texture are far superior to a mix. This is also from the Purity Flour Cookbook, circa 1947. This will make 18 average or 12 large cupcakes or a 9 inch square cake. In all cases, grease the pans, including the tops of the cupcake tins, very well. The macaroon topping can be sticky.

1/2 cup butter	1/2 tsp salt
1 tsp vanilla	1 cup milk
1 1/2 cups sugar	2 egg whites
2 eggs and 2 egg yolks	3/4 cup brown sugar, lightly packed
2 1/2 cups sifted all purpose flour	1 cup unsweetened shredded coconut
3 tsp baking powder	

Preheat oven to 350F. Cream butter until very soft, then beat in vanilla. Gradually beat in sugar until light and fluffy. Beat 2 eggs and 2 egg yolks together until light and foamy, then beat well into butter and sugar mixture. For best results, use an electric or stand mixer and beat the batter at this point for 3 to 5 minutes. This will incorporate a lot of air and help the cake be light. The batter should be pale and fluffy. Sift together flour, baking powder and salt. Now add about 1/4 of the flour and fold gently into the batter. Pour in about 1/3 of the milk and again fold gently until incorporated. Continue adding flour and milk alternately, ending with flour.

Spread the cake batter carefully into greased 9" pan, or cupcake tins. Beat 2 egg whites until stiff, and gradually beat in brown sugar. Fold in coconut and spread over cake or cupcake batter.

Bake single cake 45 to 50 minutes, bake large cupcakes 30 to 35 minutes, medium cupcakes 25 to 30 minutes.

Grant's Carrot Cake

My brother first had this cake from a friend in the 60's. He asked his friend's mother for the recipe, and I got a copy from Grant. I pass it on here with no changes. It is one of the most frequently requested recipes I have.

Cake:

2 cups sugar

2 cups all purpose flour

3 cups shredded carrots

2 tsp baking soda

1 1/4 cups vegetable oil

4 eggs

2 tsp cinnamon

pinch of salt (1/8 tsp)

2 tsp vanilla

Frosting:

8 ounce package cream cheese, room temperature and slightly warmed in the microwave

1/2 cup unsalted butter (1 stick), room temperature

1 tsp vanilla

1 tsp orange juice (this is in the original recipe, but I have successfully omitted it)

maple syrup to taste; start at 1/4 cup, and add more to your liking.

Preheat oven to 350F. Grease and flour (or line with parchment paper) one 9 x 13" or two 8 x 8" cake pans. Mix flour, soda, salt and cinnamon together in a bowl. Set aside. In a separate bowl, beat together eggs and oil until very light, then stir in carrots and vanilla. Mix in dry ingredients. Pour into one 9 x 13" or two 8 x 8" greased pans. Bake the one large pan for about 35 minutes. If using smaller pans, check around about 30 minutes for doneness. The sides of the cake should start to pull away from the pan's edge when done, and a toothpick stuck in centre will come out clean. Allow cake to cool fully before frosting.

For the frosting, blend all ingredients together and frost sides and top of cooled carrot cake.

Cake Pudding

Somehow these retro desserts keep showing up, which is good because they are nostalgic favourites and the recipes are easily lost. I do not recall where I first found this recipe, but we had it at home when I was a kid. I used to make it in my first apartment's 1 x 2 meter kitchen. This recipe produces a butterscotch sauce, but if you add cocoa to the topping, the result is a chocolate sauce.

1 cup flour

2 tsp baking powder

2/3 cup sugar

1 tsp salt

1/2 cup milk

2 tbsp melted butter

1 tsp vanilla

1 cup brown sugar

1/4 cup cocoa (add for a chocolate sauce)

1 1/2 cups boiling water

Preheat oven to 350F. Sift together flour, baking powder, sugar and salt. Add milk, butter and vanilla. Mix only until smooth. Put the cake dough in a greased pan. Sprinkle the brown sugar and cocoa (if using) over the dough. Using the back of a large spoon, pour 1 1/2 cups of boiling water over the spoon and onto the dough. Bake for 40 minutes. Serve warm.

Spanish Bar

The A & P grocery chain sold Spanish Bar as an in-house bakery item many years ago. It was a bar-shaped spice cake with white filling and icing. Bill and I started to reminisce about it one day when shopping. A & P ceased operations in 2015 and we both missed Spanish Bar. We were not alone. I found this reverse-engineered version on the internet. Many years have gone by since we had the original, but this tastes the same. I made it for a Christmas open house in 2018 and it was very popular; we barely got a piece ourselves.

This recipe will make one 9x13" cake or two double-layer bar cakes, similar to the original. I cooked the batter in 4 loaf tins and then assembled two double layer cakes with filling and icing. The icing proposed by the internet version relied on 1 cup of shortening. My alternate version is below.

Cake:

2 cups flour	1 tsp nutmeg
1 1/2 cups sugar	1 tsp allspice
1 1/2 tsp baking soda	1/2 cup vegetable oil
1 tbsp Dutch process cocoa	2 cups applesauce
1 tsp cinnamon	1 1/2 cups raisins, soaked in hot water until plumped, then drained
1 tsp salt	

Frosting:

8 ounce package cream cheese	2 1/2 cup icing sugar
4 tbsp butter (1/2 stick) (room temperature)	1/3 cup milk
2 tsp vanilla	1 tsp lemon juice

Preheat oven to 350F. Grease and flour one 9 x 15 inch pan, two 8 x 8 pans, or four loaf pans. In a large bowl, whisk all dry ingredients and spices together. In a separate bowl, beat together eggs, oil and applesauce, and then combine with dry ingredients. Add in raisins and stir to combine. Pour batter into pan(s) and rap 3 or 4 times on the counter to release air bubbles. Bake one large pan for 30 to 35 minutes; start checking small pans at 20 minutes for doneness. Cake is done when toothpick comes out of centre with only a few crumbs on it. Let cake cool completely before frosting.

To make the frosting, warm the cream cheese slightly in the microwave and beat in butter. Beat in the additional ingredients, one after another. This will fill and frost 2 two-layer bar cakes.

Boozy Hazelnut Cake

I originally clipped a version of this recipe out of Chatelaine magazine, circa 2000, from a section on Christmas Cakes. The original had hazelnuts and was soaked in Frangelico hazelnut liqueur, and I thought it was wonderful. It is a light fruitcake and the liqueur made a real difference. Unfortunately, when I offered "Christmas Fruitcake" to friends, I was not met with little cries of joy. People chose a shortbread instead and ignored the cake altogether. I then changed the recipe a little. I removed all the candied fruit and replaced it with dried fruit, and started calling it Boozy Hazelnut Cake. It was far more popular. Here's my version.

2 cups dried fruit such as golden raisins, chopped apricots and dried cranberries.

1/4 cup crystallized or candied ginger, finely chopped

1/2 cup brandy

1/2 cup Frangelico hazelnut liqueur

3 cups all purpose flour

1 cup whole hazelnuts

1/2 cup each unsalted butter and shortening (both at room temperature)

3/4 cup granulated sugar

4 eggs

2 tsp vanilla

finely grated peel of one orange (optional)

One Day Before:

Place dried fruit in a large bowl. Stir in 1/4 cup each of brandy and Frangelico. Cover and leave overnight.

The next day, make the cake:

Preheat oven to 275F. Grease one large, 9 inch spring form pan or use several smaller pans that together will hold 6 1/2 cups batter. In the past, I have purchased foil Texas Loaf size pans and made individual cakes as Christmas gifts. Line the bottom of the pan(s) with greased parchment paper. Sprinkle 1/2 cup flour over the marinated fruit and toss to coat evenly. Mix in hazelnuts. In another large bowl, beat together butter and shortening. Gradually beat in sugar, eggs and vanilla. Stir in 1/3 of remaining flour, just until mixed. Beat in the last 1/4 cup brandy, then mix in half of remaining flour, then beat in last 1/4 cup of Frangelico, then mix in remaining flour. Stir in orange peel. Pour batter over floured fruit and nut mixture and blend together. Turn into cake pan(s) and smooth the top. Bake one large pan for three hours. If you are using two loaf pans, reduce the cooking time to two hours. Reduce baking times accordingly for smaller pans. Bake until a cake tester comes out almost clean. I usually pour more Frangelico over the cake while it is still in the pan, and allow it to soak in. Making small holes over the surface with a toothpick improves the penetration of the liqueur into the cake. Remove from pan and cool on a rack until at room temperature. Wrap in brandy or Frangelico-soaked cheesecloth, then in foil. Keep refrigerated. Refresh brandy or Frangelico on the cheesecloth wrapping every two or three weeks.

Chocolate Zucchini Cake

I first made this in the 1980's when I was unexpectedly gifted with a single giant zucchini one summer. The cake is moist and chocolatey. I took it to work and it was consumed within hours.

2 1/2 cups all purpose flour	3/4 cup unsalted butter
1/2 cup cocoa	1 cup packed brown sugar
2 1/2 tsp baking powder	3 eggs
1 1/2 tsp baking soda	2 tsp grated orange rind
1 tsp salt	2 tsp vanilla
1 tsp cinnamon	2 cups grated zucchini
1 cup chopped nuts	1/2 cup milk

Preheat oven to 350F. Grease a 4 quart bundt pan. Mix flour, cocoa, baking powder, baking soda, salt, cinnamon and nuts together and set aside. In a separate bowl, cream butter and sugar together. Add beaten eggs, mixing well. Stir in orange rind, vanilla and zucchini. Add flour to batter alternately with milk, starting with flour and making 4 additions of flour and three additions of milk in total. Pour into a greased 4 quart bundt pan. Bake for about one hour.

Quark Blueberry Cheesecake

Quark is a fresh white cheese. It is creamy, high in protein and relatively low in calories. This is a less rich version of a standard cheesecake, and it is quite good.

Crust:

1 1/2 cups all purpose flour	1/4 cup butter
1/4 cup sugar	1 large egg
1 1/2 tsp baking powder	1 tsp vanilla

Filling:

1/4 cup sugar	2 tsp grated lemon rind
2 tbsp cornstarch	500 gm of quark cheese
1/4 tsp nutmeg	3 cups blueberries, fresh or frozen

Preheat oven to 325F. Grease a 10 inch spring form pan. For the crust, combine flour, sugar and baking powder. Cut in butter until mixture resembles coarse meal. In a small bowl beat together egg and vanilla. Stir into the flour mixture first with a fork, then work it in with your hands until it is thoroughly moistened. It will not hold together like a dough. Press into the bottom of the spring form pan and about half way up the side. Partially bake the crust for 10 minutes.

For the filling, mix the sugar, cornstarch and nutmeg together and stir that into the quark cheese along with the lemon rind until thoroughly combined. To assemble, spread the blueberries on the partially cooked crust. Drop the quark mixture in dollops over the blueberries and spread evenly with a knife just to the edge of the crust. Return to the oven and bake for 60 to 70 minutes until the edges of the filling are brown. Cool on a rack and serve at room temperature or chilled.

Bill's Favourite Cheesecake

I discovered that Bill loved cheesecake early on in our courtship. Since I did not know how to make cheesecake, I started experimenting. We ended up with this version, which remained his favourite recipe thereafter.

Crust:

2 cups graham wafer crumbs

1/2 cup melted butter

1 tsp cinnamon

Filling:

1 1/2 pounds cream cheese, room temperature

1 cup white sugar

2 tbsp lemon juice

1 1/2 tsp vanilla

3 eggs

Mix the crust ingredients together well. Pack about one half or more onto the bottom of a 9 inch spring form pan. Use the rest of the crumbs to line the side of the pan to form the edge. Press firmly into place using the side of a glass. Chill.

Preheat oven to 325F. Beat together the cheese and sugar until smooth and soft. Add lemon juice, vanilla, and eggs, mixing very well. Pour into the chilled crust and bake for about 45 minutes. The edge of the cheesecake should be firm, but the middle will still be soft. Turn off heat and leave the cake in the oven to cool completely. Put a fruit glaze on top if you wish.

Chocolate Cheesecake

This is a rich, over the top, dessert, best eaten by teenagers with a high metabolism.

Crust:

1 package Christie brand chocolate wafers

4 tablespoons or more melted butter

Filling:

12 ounces semi sweet chocolate chips, melted

3 eggs

1 1/2 cups sugar

3/4 cup sour cream

24 ounces (750 g) cream cheese at room temperature

Preheat the oven to 350F. For the crust, crush the crackers and add the melted butter. Press into bottom and sides of a 9 inch spring form pan. Bake for five minutes.

For the filling, mix the cream cheese and sugar together well. Add the sour cream and eggs and mix well. Add the melted chocolate to the cheese mixture, mixing well. Pour into the prepared crust. Bake for 45 minutes, until the edges are puffy and the centre is still soft. Cool and chill.

Black Forest Sheet Cake

I found this recipe online at a website called Macheesmo. I used it to make a cake to bring to work for a birthday, but omitted the bourbon and used water for the cherry preparation. The cake is straightforward to make, tasty and pretty. Nick Evans, the author of the recipe and the website, describes it as "a rich (but easy to make) chocolate sheet cake topped with loads of sweet cherries, whipped cream, and shaved chocolate."

Cake:

2 cups all purpose flour	1 tsp vanilla
1 1/2 cups sugar	2 large eggs
1/4 tsp salt	1 cup unsalted butter
1/2 cup buttermilk	1/4 cup cocoa powder
1 tsp baking soda	1 cup boiling water

Cherries:

24 ounces frozen pitted cherries, thawed (or one can halved cherries)	1/2 cup sugar
	1 tablespoon bourbon (optional)

Whipping Cream:

2 cups whipping cream	2 tbsp sugar
1 tsp vanilla	shaved chocolate, or dark chocolate chips, to garnish

Preheat oven to 350F. Grease a 9x13 sheet pan. In a small saucepan, melt butter over medium low heat. Stir in cocoa powder. When butter has melted, stir in boiling water and let bubble for a few minutes over medium heat. Remove from heat. In a large bowl, whisk together flour, sugar, and salt. In a separate smaller bowl, whisk together buttermilk, eggs, vanilla and baking soda.

Pour chocolate mixture into flour mixture and whisk together. Then stir in the buttermilk and egg mixture. Mix until batter is smooth and then pour into a 12 x 12 or 9 x 13 sheet pan. Bake cake for 20 minutes until a tester comes out clean from the centre.

While the cake is baking, combine cherries, sugar, and bourbon (if using; I substituted water) in a pot over low heat. Once sugar is dissolved and cherries are steaming, remove from heat and let cool. When cake is done, spoon cherry mixture over the top of the cake. Let the cake cool to room temperature before adding whipped cream.

Whisk together whipped cream with vanilla and sugar and spread evenly over cooled chocolate cake. Garnish with shaved chocolate or chocolate chips.

Fruit Crumble

This is a flexible recipe from my friend Joyce. You can alter the type and amount of fruit, and the thickening agent. Every time I make this, someone comments on how good it is. I think part of it is the simplicity of the recipe.

4 cups (or more) fruit, such as apples, peaches, plums

2 heaping tbsp cornstarch or tapioca powder

1/2 cup sugar

a pinch of salt (1/8 tsp)

1 to 2 tbsp butter

1/2 cup sugar

1 egg

1/2 cup all purpose flour

1 tsp baking powder

Preheat oven to 350F. Mix together cornstarch (or tapioca), 1/2 cup sugar and a pinch of salt. Toss with fruit and pour into a greased 8 x 8 inch pan, or a similar sized casserole dish. In a separate bowl, blend together butter with sugar. Stir in a beaten egg, then add flour and baking powder. Drop by spoonfuls over fruit, and smooth out with the back of the spoon. Bake about 45 minutes.

Fruit Tray

This isn't a recipe, but simply a method.

For the fruit, either cut up fresh fruit such as pineapple, melon and lay out on a a tray with berries, such as strawberries and blueberries

OR

skewer the fruit on sticks, which makes eating easier and reduces the dipping of sticky bits into the dips

Make two dips for the fruit, and put in small pots on the fruit tray. For the first dip, take one single serving of vanilla yogurt, and stir in a couple spoonfuls of raspberry preserves.

For the second dip, buy a can of ready-made Devon Custard. In Canada, you can buy it at the Loblaw's chain of stores. Failing that, make up the filling for Graham Wafer Pie (chapter 9). Put some custard in a chilled pot and put on the fruit tray.

If the fruit tray is going to sit out in the summer heat for any period of time, do not use custard made from scratch.

Chapter 11

Miscellany

Basil Pesto

I love basil pesto, and like to have some in the freezer as part of the basic larder, like tomato sauce in a jar. This recipe for pesto is simple and delicious. Most summers, I grow several basil bushes in the garden just so I can make fresh pesto. Basil is better harvested when the plant is young; older leaves turn bitter. This recipe came from a tag on a bunch of fresh basil.

2 cups packed fresh basil leaves

2 cloves garlic

1/4 cup pine nuts

2/3 cup extra-virgin olive oil, divided

coarse salt and freshly ground black pepper, to taste

1/2 cup freshly grated Pecorino or Parmesan cheese

Combine the basil, garlic and pine nuts in a food processor and pulse until coarsely chopped. Add 1/2 cup of the oil slowly with the machine running and process until fully incorporated and smooth. Season with salt and pepper.

If using immediately, add all the remaining oil and pulse until smooth. Transfer the pesto to a large serving bowl and mix in the cheese, salt and pepper.

If freezing, transfer to an airtight container and drizzle remaining oil over the top. Freeze for up to 3 months. Thaw and stir in cheese, salt and pepper.

Ricardo's Green Tomato Jam

After a hot and dry growing season, I had a late crop of green tomatoes that did not ripen. I picked them and made this jam. The recipe is from Ricardo's website. The jam is mildly spicy, but has no tomato flavour. I had not done any canning before, so I used new jars and froze them three quarters full.

12 cups diced green tomatoes, about 5lb

2 MacIntosh apples, peeled, seeded, cored and diced

6 cups sugar

1/2 cup lemon juice

In a heavy saucepan, combine all the ingredients. Bring to a gentle boil, stirring frequently. Attach a candy thermometer in the centre of the pan and simmer for about 1 hour and 15 minutes or until the thermometer reads 104 C (219 F). Skim carefully and stir frequently while cooking. Pour into sterilized jars and store in refrigerator or freezer.

Rhubarb Chutney

adapted from *The Spruce Eats* website

This spring friends gave me a bunch of fresh rhubarb from their garden. In the past I usually paired it with strawberries and made pie. I did not have strawberries on hand, so I went online and found this recipe. The simplicity really appealed to me, as I am new to putting things up in jars. Everyone that has tried this chutney has liked it a lot. Make sure to put some up in smaller jars that you can give to friends who taste it.

5 cups rhubarb, chopped in 1/2 inch pieces

5 cups white sugar

3 cups sultanas or raisins

2 cups white vinegar

1 ounce/ 25 gm salt (scant 2 tbsp)

1 ounce / 25 gm powdered ginger (scant 2 tbsp)

1 finely chopped onion

Put all ingredients into a pot, and bring to a boil. Turn down the heat to a simmer. Let cook about one hour, until reduced, thick and dark. It will make a "plopping" sound as it cooks. Stir occasionally. Pour into clean, sterilized jars. Store in the refrigerator.

Buffet Meatball Sauce

I remember having meatballs at a party that were sauced with a mixture of grape jelly and canned gravy, and everyone loved them. Subsequent research online revealed a trend: a good sauce for a buffet or cocktail meatball is half jam or jelly and half savoury liquid like a gravy or broth. Voila.

So here is what I made up.

Mix equal amounts of tomato jam and beef broth in a pan. I have used 1 1/2 cups each with good results. If you use more, increase the amounts of corn starch and water. Mix the jam and broth together and bring to a boil. Mix together 2 tbsp. cornstarch and 2 tbsp. water, stir into boiling jam mixture, stir and cook until mixture is thickened and glossy. Warm pre-cooked meatballs, pour sauce over, and set out for buffet.

Hummus

2 tins chickpeas, drained and rinsed

2 garlic cloves

Juice of one lemon

1/4 cup olive oil

In a blender, process the olive oil, lemon juice and garlic cloves until blended. Gradually work in the chickpeas until it becomes a fine paste.

Apple Cider Syrup

This can be used as a sweetener in apple pie or cobbler.

Take sweet apple cider and measure it. The aim is to reduce it to 1/4 of this volume. Four cups should reduce to one cup. Over medium high heat, bring cider to a boil and then reduce to a low simmer. Simmer for about 1 hour 20 minutes or until the cider has reduced by about ¾ and coats a spoon.

Optional: pour through a wire mesh strainer lined with cheesecloth to remove the sediment. Use immediately or refrigerate for up to a week.

Margaritas

One can of frozen limeade

One bottle of beer

Ice, enough to fill limeade tin

Tequila, enough to fill limeade tin

Allow frozen limeade to thaw. Pour into blender. Fill up the empty can with ice cubes, then empty into the blender. Fill up the empty can with tequila and pour in the blender. Fill up the empty can with beer and pour in the blender. Hold the lid firmly on the blender, and process on high until the ice cubes are crushed. Serve.

Sweet Blintz or Crepe

3/4 cup flour	2 eggs
1/2 tsp salt	2/3 cup milk
1 tsp baking powder	1 cup water
2 tbsp powdered sugar	1/2 tsp vanilla

Beat eggs, add milk, water and vanilla. Blend together dry ingredients. Stir wet ingredients into dry ingredients. There may be lumps, do not worry. Leave the batter to sit for one hour in the refrigerator and the lumps will disappear. Fry 1/4 to 1/3 cup batter in a hot 7 or 8 inch greased cast iron pan. Cook until edges are dry, flip and cook about 30 seconds longer.

Granola

This is adapted from Alton Brown's recipe on the *Food Network* website. You can change the nuts, fruit and sweetener as the larder dictates.

3 cups rolled oats

2 cups mixed types of nuts, unsalted and raw; I often used 2 cups of walnuts

3/4 cup shredded unsweetened coconut

1/4 cup plus 2 tbsp maple syrup

1/4 cup vegetable oil

1 tsp cinnamon

3/4 tsp salt

1 cup raisins or mixed fruit, up to 1 cup total

Preheat oven to 250F. In a large bowl combine oats, nuts and coconut. In a separate bowl mix maple syrup, oil, cinnamon and salt. Combine both mixtures and toss well to coat everything. Pour onto 2 ungreased rimmed sheet pans. Cook for 1 hour and 15 minutes, stirring every 15 minutes for even toasting. Remove from oven and transfer to large bowl. Add dried fruit. Mix well. Store in airtight containers.